Tarheel Hilarities

a

Collection of Humor

by

Warren Dixon, Jr.

FIVE HAWKS   Five Hawks Press   Liberty, NC

ISBN 0-9648321-0-0

Library of Congress Number 95-90674

Printed in the USA by Greensboro Printing

Cover and book design by Joyce Parham Design

Five Hawks Press
P.O. Box 1203
Liberty, N.C. 27298

To My Wife

Sandra

Without Whom
There Could Be No Book

"For me, it is to laugh."

O. Henry

Acknowledgements

All of the stories and columns in this book were published elsewhere in one form or another. Many have been combined or re-written for publication here.

The stories "A Package Marked 'Agile'" and "Breathing Can Be Habit Forming" first appeared in *Postal Life*. "My Money Log", "The Handy Man Can" and "Yule Log" were published in *Carolina Country*. "Grandma's Christmas Riches" appeared in *The State*. "Squirrel Wars", although it had its debut in *The Liberty* (N.C.) *News*, was also published in *Wildlife in North Carolina*. The now de-funct *Villager* (Liberty, N.C.) first printed "And They Call It A 'Festival'." "Burned on the Fourth of July", "Litters of Critters", "Listening License" and "Christmas is Giving" first appeared in *The Bulletin* (Ramseur, N.C.). All other columns and stories were initially printed in *The Liberty News*. All are reprinted here with permission of the editors of these fine publications.

Although the writer ultimately writes the book, no one does it alone. My deepest thanks goes to:

My wife Sandra, who makes me laugh, and who makes my writing possible; Sims Poindexter, my wonderful tenth grade English teacher at Jordan Matthews High School, for discovering my talent and encouraging me; the late Chub Seawell of Carthage, N.C., who unknowingly gave me my style; my cousin Glenn Wells of Bostic, N.C., and my old childhood pal, Richard Wentworth of Charlotte, both of whom introduced me to Willard; my father, the late Dewey Dixon and my mother, Bertene Dixon of Siler City, for buying me books, putting up with my writing late at night and for sending me to Carolina; the late Kenneth R. Byerly, Professor of Journalism at Carolina, for teaching me more about writing in one semester than I've learned since; the English professors Core, husband and wife team at Carolina, for much encouragement; good friend Conrad "Buck" Paysour, fishing author, for suggesting the title and for much good sound advice; good friends Henry King, author, and Chip Womick, editor, for help and advice; the late David Allen, friend and editor of *The Liberty News*, for always printing anything I turned in; my stepdaughters Julie and Jamie McCoy and close friends Susan and Walt Foster, Peggy and Ed Christenbury, Peggy Stanford and Bud Davis, and Willard and Hoyle, for letting me write about them and still speaking to me; Charlie Bowen, for financial advice; Joyce Parham, for lots of technical advice and design skills; also a special thanks to Jim Chilton, Steve Sugg, Wynne Troy, Raeford Morgan, Phil Pollet and Wade Lowe.

Preface

There are many reasons a writer publishes a book. Insanity would be one. Another would be a latent urge to go bankrupt. But I have only one reason for putting this book together: I like to hear people laugh.

A friend once asked me to teach her how to write humor. I studied it awhile and came to the conclusion that I don't know how I write humor. It's a God given talent, one that I've failed to improve on much since I first began to write in Miss Ruth Smith's seventh grade class. This did not endear me to Miss Smith, by the way, especially since I wrote *during* her class. It didn't help matters any, either, when Richard Wentworth gave an oral book report on the unfinished novel.

Humor is a fragile commodity. You walk a fine line when you write humor, because not everyone sees with the same eyes. You can easily offend someone if you're not careful and I try to do this every now and then. I don't believe in letting sleeping dogs lie. I like to poke one now and then and see what he'll do. I don't mind taking a shot at a sacred cow every once in awhile, either. Sometimes you get a good filet out of it.

Humor can be a powerful tool, but mainly its purpose is to make you laugh. I've found that the more you study humor, the less funny it becomes. So, I say just sit back and enjoy it.

In spite of the fact that Sandra says the truth is not in me, a great many parts of some of the stories in *Tarheel Hilarities* are partially based on fact. The rest are out and out lies. By the way, I say the truth is in me, it just rarely comes out.

The forty stories contained in this book constitute my favorites over the years. It took me a long time to agree with all my teachers that it's best to write about something familiar to you. Readers can identify with painting a house or trimming a Christmas tree or fighting off a horde of devious squirrels and see the humor in the folly of it all. Life is a lot more fun when you can laugh about it and believe me, there is plenty to laugh about at our house.

North Carolina humorist Chub Seawell probably said it best in *Sir Walter: Earl of Chatham*:

"Some folks don't have any better sense than to write a book, but this book is written to cheer you up."

I certainly hope that *Tarheel Hilarities* cheers you up.

Contents

The Curse of the Lawn

"Don't you think the yard needs reseeding?" Sandra asked.

It was one of those rhetorical questions wives ask now and then to enliven conversation during commercial breaks in The Game of the Week. It was much like the time she mentioned, off the cuff, that the utility room might need cleaning out when in fact I knew that the utility room was actually cleaned out in 1969 and could, in no way, shape or form, need cleaning out now.

So there was no reason to think she could be serious about the yard. As a matter of fact, the yard was about as perfect as a yard could be, having the main two prerequisites for the ideal yard: just alive enough to have a greenish tint, yet dead enough that it rarely needed mowing.

All our neighbors' yards tended to look alike, tropical, dense, luxurious green grass which required mowing at ridiculously frequent intervals, some as often as once a week.

Our yard had more of a personality of its own. The back yard had the most personality, sort of the Miss Congeniality of yards. There was a nice lush carpet of chickweed there, some ground ivy, wild strawberries, honey-suckle, some scattered thistle, plantain, lamb's quarter, knotweed, pokeberry and a healthy stand of dandelion. Mostly, though, it was full of wild violets which, in the spring, bloomed purple. There was a sprinkling of an undetermined variety of grass in the far corner, but not enough to deter from the charm.

The yard on one side of the house was occupied with Bermuda Grass, so named because it originally came to America from Bermuda by burrowing all the way underground, coming up for air only once in an asphalt parking lot in Wilmington. The other side of the yard was dominated by wild onions and the aforementioned wild violets.

The front yard did not have quite the character of the back, through no fault of my own. It seems that while our neighbor was having his lawn reseeded one year, a freak wind storm blew a mixture of grass seed and fertil-izer into our yard. The landscaper apologized profusely and cleaned it up quicker than an oil spill. Still, that part of the yard was greener and thicker than the rest and required mowing much more often than I thought nec-essary. There were still enough wild violets in the front to keep it from being absolutely boring, though.

This was a yard which needed no tinkering, except maybe for the part which was mistakenly fertilized. But it definitely didn't need reseeding.

"I talked to the landscaping man today," Sandra casually continued, just as though she hadn't heard a word I'd been thinking. "He said he could reseed the yard this fall."

"Reseed?" I mumbled. "What else could we plant in it? The only plant life we're lacking is Kudzu and I expect an influx of that the first thing next summer. Just the other day the neighbors remarked enviously that we must have every weed known to mankind in our yard. Besides, that's the same landscaping guy who spilled fertilizer in our front yard and nearly ruined it. A man who uses fertilizer is not to be trusted."

We continued this engaging banter for quite some time. Finally through the use of reverse psychology, offering to reverse the daily process in which she cooks and I eat, Sandra persuaded me to her point of view. I was so persuaded that when she mentioned the price the landscaper was going to charge to reseed the lawn, I readily volunteered to do it myself.

This warmed the cockles of Sandra's heart, the cockles being the part that, when warmed, cause either great gales of laughter or intense sobbing to ensue. I could readily tell it was sobbing this time even though the sound was muffled by the locked bathroom door. No doubt she was overwhelmed by emotion that I would take on such a task by myself.

I wasted no time in riding down to the lawn and garden center. The clerk there, being familiar with our lawn, first recommended that we sell the place and move. Finally he suggested the economy size broadleaf weed killer, a sprayer and a fertilizer and seed spreader, which coming in fifty or so pieces, required some minor assembly.

The weed killer, he said, would kill only the weeds and not harm the lawn, a statement that confused me somewhat since in our yard, the weeds were the lawn.

I went home and stored the seed spreader in the utility room for later assembly. Then I hooked the sprayer to the hose, set the dial on "one" and sprayed the entire lawn.

A week later the back yard looked like the Gobi Desert. The chickweed had melted into black lumps. The dandelions had curled up. The clover was gone. As far as I could tell, the only plant that had survived, besides a little grass, was the hardy wild violet. I turned the dial to "two" and let the violets have it. A week later and they were still thriving. I turned the dial to "four" and sprayed them again. Another week and not only were the wild violets still living, but new violets were appearing where the chickweed had once grown. I went back to the lawn and garden center.

If that didn't kill the violets, said the clerk, the only thing that would was the highly concentrated grass and weed killer, which would kill anything it touched and had even been known to kill an occasional wild onion. But, he added, logically, if you're going to reseed your lawn, you don't mind killing off your grass.

I purchased a container of about a cup full which sold for slightly more a pint than plasma.

With a small spray bottle I sprayed each violet individually with weed killer, hoping to save what grass I had left. In a few days, the violets began to crinkle. The ones that didn't got an extra dose.

A week later and the entire yard was dead. Neighbors stopped by enviously wanting to know how I did it, would it spread to their yards and had I ever been sued. The Dakota Badlands had more greenery than our lawn.

"We're about ready for the next step," I proudly announced to Sandra.

"What's that?" she asked. "Putting together the seed and fertilizer spreader before the warranty expires?"

"No," I answered, "finding the seed spreader. It's in the utility room somewhere. That place really needs cleaning out."

"Aren't you going to kill all the wild violets first?" she asked.

I looked outside. Sure enough, all over the yard, little green heart-shaped leaves were sticking up through the barren soil. The wild violets had survived. A few more days and they would need mowing.

I began digging them up. They had tuber-like roots just under the ground and I threw them by the handfuls into the graveled driveway. A week later and I noticed they were taking root in the driveway. There must have been a million wild violets, all over the yard. This time when I dug them up, I was careful to throw them in the trash. Let the landfill worry with them, I thought.

October, the month the lawn and garden man had said to reseed, was creeping nearer and nearer. I kept digging up wild violets. One night I dreamed of the Return of the Curse of the Wild Violets, when wild violets survived a nuclear attack and took over New York City. I picked all the tassels off the bedspread that night.

I was getting worried. Fall was here and I still hadn't put together the seed spreader. One good rain and our yard was going to erode into the sea. The neighbors were starting to picket my house. It was obvious that I had no choice but to turn to professional help.

I called my friend Willard. Willard was qualified to work on lawns because he had known a guy who had once lived beside a man whose nephew had been in the landscaping business. He not only had the expertise, he also had one major advantage: he was free.

Sure enough, Willard went right to work. He rented an aerator and a seed spreader (mine having been lost in the utility room) and bought some seed and fertilizer.

"Looks like it would have been a lot cheaper just to

hire a landscaper," he noted.

Finally the yard was reseeded. Willard finished it up one day and had the sprinkler on when I got home from work. I surveyed his handiwork.

"What's that in the back yard?" I asked him, noticing something green under the trees.

"Oh, that's the ground cover," he said. "It's so shady back there it's hard to get anything to grow. So I set out some wild violets."

It was either the crazed look in my eyes or my hands around Willard's throat that led Willard to believe he ought to elaborate on his statement.

"They were free," he yelled, as I chased him around the yard. "I dug them up at the landfill. There were millions of them there. They bloom purple in the spring."

Family Reunions

No one knows for sure how the first family reunion came about. Archaeologists have unearthed the skeleton of Cro-Magnon man in France along side several picnic tables and what appears to be plastic milk jugs containing iced tea residue. Old Cro seems to have died from acute indigestion after consuming fifteen deviled eggs, probably Pterodactyl.

North Carolinians caught on to the tradition of family reunions early. Sir Walter Raleigh wrote of attending a family reunion near Snow Camp and noted that "the Potato Salat was rite Tasty, but filled with Pesky Nats."

Later, during the Revolution, the North Carolina Militia developed a sudden urge to return home for various family reunions upon seeing an inordinate number of British bayonets at what was to be the Battle of Guilford Courthouse. This, of course, gave rise to our now famous motto: "First in Flight."

And during the Civil War, General Robert E. Lee remarked that he found it strange that so many family reunions seemed to be scheduled right before major battles.

"It wouldn't be so bad," Lee lamented, "but the boys take all our softball equipment home with them, too."

My family was no different when it came to reunions, believing in the need to come together regularly to renew our kinship, reminisce about old times and attempt to collect bad checks. Or, as Dad said fondly, "once a year is still too often."

It was always a major problem in our family to find someone to host these annual affairs. My kinfolks were an unassuming bunch, humble and modest, and always insisted that someone else accommodate the family reunion.

One year everyone got together and approached Uncle George about holding the event at his house.

"Since you missed the last reunion," Dad explained to him, "we unanimously voted to hold the next one at your house."

"If," Dad continued, while various aunts tried their hand at fanning Uncle George back to consciousness, "we could have raised enough money we could have rented the Legion Hut, which not only has more space, but also has a bomb shelter to store all the kids."

Uncle George made a miraculous recovery and with the speed to a gravel truck on I-40, reached into his pocket and produced enough money to rent the Legion Hut with some left over to pay part of any damages incurred.

The only drawback to holding the reunion in the Legion Hut was that we all had to meet inside. This revealed a little known family flaw, recognized as the phobia of rain at family reunions or the morbid dread of being in closed rooms or narrow spaces with close kin.

After the fiasco at the Legion Hut, the reunion began to be alternated among aunts and uncles on an alphabetical basis. If memory serves me right, this was about the time Uncle George had his name legally changed to Zenobia Xavier.

We cousins always looked forward to family reunions with the enthusiasm of Pharaoh frog gigging on the Nile.

It was always fun to see other cousins and to beat them up. It took longer to renew our friendship with our despised city cousins, but soon they were beating us up just like we'd been pals for years.

Once before a reunion at Uncle Herbert's we overheard a conversation that made our hair in our ears stand straight up.

"I mean it," Uncle Herbert told Dad, "I do not want those little hoodlums running in and out of my house all day."

All week long my brother and I readied ourselves for the reunion and for the hoodlums who were going to crash our festivities. When the fateful day arrived, we patrolled Uncle Herbert's house faithfully, armed with BB guns and watching carefully for any criminals as we marched in and out of his house.

Dad finally suggested that we go outside and shoot each other as Uncle Herbert was evidently losing his gourd and was mumbling something like "if someone doesn't tie up those hoodlums and get them out of my house I'm going crazy." We always figured Uncle Herbert was "seeing things."

The focal point of all family reunions, of course, is food. That is unless someone like your Uncle Floyd has run off with someone young enough to be his granddaughter, then that takes precedence.

Food at family reunions is usually spread outside on long tables under trees or anywhere great numbers of flies congregate. Traditional reunion fare consists of potato salad, deviled eggs, green beans, fried chicken, lots of iced tea and various desserts sprinkled liberally with yellow jackets and stink bugs.

Then there's the obligatory broccoli souffle, rumored to have given Uncle Floyd the dry heaves in 1975 even after he had drunk fourteen beers.

Aunt Maude's desserts were always favorites with us, but because of their popularity you had to be quick to get one. One year we spotted one of her raisin cakes at the end of one table and made a mad dash for it while the adults were busying themselves with vegetables. By the time we reached it, though, most of the raisins had flown off leaving a surprisingly plain cake with some vanilla icing. Most of us were able to eat three or four slices with little competition from the grownups except for my younger brother who was busy trying to find which lime jello his tree frog had escaped to.

Conversation in the food line usually went something like this at our reunions:

"I wonder who brought the beef: Is that Maude's beef or Aunt Jolene's?"

"I don't know, I'm sort of afraid of it, myself. What if it's Maude's? Is that cat hair in the corn? You know it's Cat World at Aunt Jolene's. Lets them up on the table and all just like they was family."

"I bet that Luke bought that chicken at Kentucky Fried Chicken. He can't cook. Put it in one of his bowls like he fried it himself."

"I'm going to try some of this pretty Watergate salad. Or is it macaroni and cheese?"

We cousins always avoided choices like these and headed directly for the chicken legs which were hard to mistake for anything else unless perhaps it was Aunt

Maude's chocolate pecan logs.

The reunion immediately following Uncle Floyd's escape with the younger woman was particularly interesting to us kids. We couldn't wait to quiz him on this phenomenon and had formed a gauntlet of cousins to meet him when he arrived.

Being of equestrian persuasion myself, I was interested in where Uncle Floyd was keeping this new filly we had overheard Dad talking about. In particular, I wanted to ask Uncle Floyd the origin of the phrase "hot to trot."

My younger brother was curious about any jail sentence incurred for robbing the cradle and, if Uncle Floyd was as tight with a dollar as Dad said, why would he feel the need to steal.

After we had approached Uncle Floyd with these questions, we had our first exposure to the words "jerk a knot in your tail." It struck me immediately that this must have been the fate of the poor Hunchback of Notre Dame, who as a healthy young lad had probably questioned his uncle one too many times on horse related matters.

This response from our uncle so frightened my brother that he leaped under the steering wheel of our car and balled up underneath the dashboard like a squirrel, causing the turn signals to permanently malfunction. He later apologized, saying he'd been taken back momentarily, never having seen a grown man foam at the mouth.

It wasn't until years later when we visited Uncle Floyd that I realized our mistake in interrogating him. The poor man didn't even own a barn much less a horse which explained why he was always so short with us.

Our family reunions always ended with a game of some sort. We surmised this was the womenfolks idea to keep the men out of any clean-up activities.

Our favorite game was football, the object of which was to render our uncles totally incapable of ever doing manual labor again.

The uncle's favorite play consisted of a sweep around the right side of the line, a position manned by Uncle Bubba. This was always followed by a timeout and a trip to the iced tea pitcher.

Several uncles always attempted to weasel out of these games with lame excuses such as they "might ruin their good shoes" or they needed all their ribs intact for their jobs Monday morning. Because of this we always played barefooted, except for the year we played in the cow pasture, and we made it a five yard penalty for breaking anyone's ribs.

Finally one year Uncle Charlie put an end to these games by announcing that Lloyd's of London had failed to renew his football insurance and that sadly he could no longer participate. Later Mom told us that Uncle Charlie would possibly be able to walk again once the bones in his toes knitted and the doctors removed the cast.

Afterwards we played softball at these reunions, but it wasn't the same bone crushing fun as football had been. We let Uncle Floyd be permanent pitcher for both sides since Dad said he stayed pretty whipped most of the time anyway.

Normally we played until someone lost the ball, which usually occurred soon after Mom announced that there was some banana pudding left over if anyone wanted it.

This annual softball game ended suddenly one afternoon when Uncle George hit a 450 yard shot over Rocky River and beat it out for a single. When he finally caught his breath, he led a mutiny to his pickup truck where all the uncles finished the day in the shade listening to the car race on the radio.

The next year the uncles were seen lugging a checker board to the reunion. Uncle Herbert said he'd ruined enough good shoes at family reunions to be able to buy hip replacements, have his knees put back into the sockets and have enough left over to recap his shins and he was through with contact sports.

This was fine with us cousins because by this time in our lives we had discovered girls although there was some disagreement among us over what to do with them. Some of us wanted to let them play softball with us and others wanted to shoot them with BB guns.

We all had to agree, though, that these family reunions had left their mark on all of us, one that Dad assured us would undoubtedly heal over time.

Deep Sea Fishing, Or, What Goes Down Must Come Up

It was going to be, or so Willard promised, more fun than the Coca Cola 600. Hoyle agreed. Deep sea fishing, he said, beat auto racing hands down.

If deep sea fishing was any more exciting than Charlotte Motor Speedway's Coca Cola 600, I didn't know if I could handle the excitement. I remembered the fun we had that day at the speedway because I still suffered from partial deafness, a condition brought on from sitting all afternoon three feet away from a spot where at any given time forty mufflerless cars were going around in circles at 200 miles an hour.

That was the day Willard had purchased us the best tickets his money and considerable influence could buy. We sat about three rows from the race track in seats unencumbered by any shade. It was not unlike sitting on the center stripe on Interstate 40 just outside Winston Salem, except that the trucks on I-40 would have been going faster.

Right after the sun had broiled us to a bright pink, we became covered with a thick coat of tire dust and road grime, looking much like Nutty Buttys. By this time we really didn't care because the persistent roar somewhat akin to the space shuttle going off next door had numbed us to anything.

We were just close enough to the track to get splattered when fans threw beer cans over the fence at their favorite drivers. We were also downwind of the restrooms, which were conveniently located two miles away. There, at any given moment, 20,000 people stood in line, some of them actually sober.

Sometime before the race was over, we headed for the car. Willard said you could beat the traffic that way, most of whom thought they were Richard Petty at a demolition derby. Besides, he said, you could hear who won the race on the radio. I suggested next time we just sit in Willard's car and listen to the race on the radio, but Willard said that would ruin all the fun. Hoyle did promise, however, to remember to bring ear plugs the next time we went to a race.

So, with a deep sea fishing expedition promising to be more enjoyable than a day at the race, how could a guy refuse?

Hoyle had seen in the paper where someone had caught a two-ton Marlin off the coast near Morehead and he was determined to catch one himself and mount it in the garage. Hoyle's wife had told him years ago not to bring any fish in the house that wasn't already fried with hush puppies and french fries, so Hoyle had plans to mount his over the washer and drier, a place Willard said he spent most of his time anyway.

We took my car to the coast, as usual. I always drove on expeditions like this so Hoyle and Willard could sleep on the way down. This way they were alert enough when we reached our destination to stay awake all night and to wake me up in case I dozed off accidently, say, at 3:00 in the morning.

Willard had purchased us, so he said, the best accommodations his money and considerable influence could buy at the coast. We arrived in Morehead late that Friday night and followed a wharf rat family to our cabin. I thought the pile of fish heads outside our window would keep me awake all night, but Willard and Hoyle did instead. We were lucky the place had screened in windows. This trapped all the mosquitoes inside and allowed us to sit unbothered on the porch all night.

Sometime early in the morning Hoyle cooked us ham and eggs and grits swimming in grease. The grease, he claimed, was good to settle your stomach once you got out on the open sea. He'd forgotten to bring the sea sick pills, but said real men didn't need them anyway. He had, however, remembered to bring the ear plugs.

I spotted our boat just as soon as we pulled up to the dock. It was the Lusitania ll. The skipper was patching holes in the hull from the last torpedo attack.

I knew I was in trouble as soon as land disappeared from sight. The boat was going one way, the horizon the other and my stomach was perpendicular to both of them. Hoyle had just commented on what a nice shade of pale I had turned when my breakfast, in the best tradition of the loaves and fishes, went forth and multiplied.

Willard wondered if I could come aft and hang overboard, thinking I might attract some really big fish. It had never occurred to me that a day could last so long. I remember asking Captain Ahab if he could drop me off at the pier. He promised he would later that afternoon, which I figured was about a week away.

Sometime around hour 56 of my ordeal, I looked up from my perspective on the deck and saw Willard reel in a pretty big fish.

"It doesn't get any better than this," he whooped.

I began to plan how best to kill Willard without anyone finding out. I would stab him with a harpoon, several of which I was certain Captain Ahab kept aboard. Then I would throw him overboard where the sharks would surely devour the evidence.

But, knowing my luck, Willard's carcass would wash ashore where Jerry Bledsoe would find it and write a best-seller about the murder. This was the only thing that saved Willard's hide.

We docked late that afternoon shortly after I promised the powers-that-be for the third time never to go near water, eggs, fish or Willard again.

Of course, I drove us home so that Hoyle and Willard could sleep. But just before they dozed off, Willard told me about flounder gigging.

Flounder gigging, he said, was more fun than deep sea fishing. Hoyle agreed. Flounder gigging, he said, beat deep sea fishing hands down. You waded out into the sound waist deep around midnight and sometimes it rained and sometimes the lightning popped and sometimes your boat got stuck on sand bars for hours at a time. It was terrible fun because you had a light in one hand and a gig in the other and you stabbed these flounder and sometimes each other.

I wondered on the way home after they had gone to sleep if it really would be so bad to have Jerry Bledsoe write a book about you after all.

The Handy Man Can

The wife and I agreed unanimously one to zero recently that I would paint the house. It was not a challenge I took lightly, having come from a long line of "do-it-yourselfers", most of whom had still not returned the tools they had borrowed from me last year.

There is nothing more reassuring than the knowledge that you can do it yourself, unless of course it is the knowledge that your brother-in-law is a plumber and owes you innumerable favors. There is a lot of pride involved in knowing that for a few thousand dollars and a scant month or two of your time you can do basically the same job a professional could do in a couple of hours for less money.

A short, concise history of our country shows us why we Americans are such natural jacks of all trades. America was settled by fiercely individualistic pioneers who insisted on doing all home repairs themselves, with the exception of rebuilding carburetors, which luckily for them had not yet been invented. These early settlers became jacks of all trades out of necessity, being so isolated that help often took weeks to arrive, much like the response time of our modern day plumbers.

The frontiers are gone now, but today's do-it-yourselfers epitomize the American democratic spirit, independent nature and refusal to admit defeat even when faced with the overwhelming odds of a clogged drainpipe. Home repair and maintenance has now become so complicated that entire industries have built up around the phenomenon, including homeowner's insurance, emergency medical response teams and divorce lawyers.

All this provides today's handyman with an interesting challenge. To handle this, the modern day do it yourselfer has a wide range of tools available to him, most of which are in the trunk of his brother-in-law's car at this very moment.

Having the right tools is the first rule of the expert handyman. For instance, a look into my tool box reveals the following:

*a lead pencil, no lead

*a jackknife, handy for sharpening pencil, cleaning under fingernails or for use as a screwdriver. Dull enough as not to cut user, or much else for that matter.

*assorted loose change. Dimes and quarters make good screwdrivers in case knife is not available. Pennies can also be used in place of fuses (see section on fire insurance)

*standard screwdriver. Can be used as a chisel or to open paint cans. Every tool box will have one of these, especially if the job requires a Phillips head screwdriver (named appropriately after the Milk of Magnesia taken after stripping several screw heads)

*435 nuts, bolts, screws and nails, all of which are either too long, too short, too big or too small for normal use.

*box of Band-Aids. Indispensable to today's handyman (see also section on saws)

*flashlight, with something brown oozing from one end.

*assorted lengths of string and wire, suitably tangled.

*empty sealant tube.

*glob of something resembling sealant with Allen wrench, breath mint and partial roll of electrical tape stuck in it.

*fingernail clippers, good for cutting wire.

In addition to these few basic tools, the average handyman will also need a good curved claw hammer (for pulling out bent nails). For plumbing chores, it is recommended that you have a good plunger on hand and a pair of knee boots.

The second rule of the do-it-yourselfer is preventative maintenance. This is the most rewarding part of the handyman's work, for it extends the life of not only the home, but also tools and equipment, most of which come with basically the same warranty as fly larvae.

Take lawn mowers for instance. Our household has two push mowers, considerably more push mowers than mowees, but then another good rule of having machinery is to keep spares. Good maintenance on mowers means adding oil occasionally, changing spark plugs once one gets black, and scrapping dried grass from the underside of the mower. Preventative maintenance such as this will keep your mower going two-three years.

Maintaining electrical appliances presents a particular obstacle to the budding handyman. To be certain of the safety of appliances and fixtures, you should always look for the UL listing. This stands, of course, for Union Label and insures that you aren't purchasing some scab product. Basic rules for working with electricity are two-fold. You need to know where the circuit breaker is located and how to call the local fire department.

The last, but one of the most important, rules of handymanship is to keep a detailed log of everything done around the house. My log consists of several well-worn notebooks filled with detailed information on home improvements, scores of Carolina games and dates of tetanus shots.

A log can prove valuable in many ways. You can keep track of supplies purchased, equipment used, jobs you've begun and the dates they were finally completed by professionals.

The log is also handy in answering certain questions that may come up concerning repairs, as when the plumber asks "who wrenched this shower head off its threads?" or in court when the lawyer wants to know "what brand of mortar did you use on the defective steps that broke under the considerable weight of said plaintiff?"

A quick glance at the log, in these cases, will reveal that the pages in question have been inexplicably jerked out of the book.

To help the occasional do-it-yourselfer better understand the workings of a handyman's log, I have included a excerpt from mine here. This particular section concerns the aforementioned subject of painting, which the wife agreed that I would do as soon as possible:

April 21: Wife suggests exterior of house may need painting merely because it's beginning to peel. I tell her that to save money, I will do it myself. Wife requests to know approximate date job will begin. I tell her that I will get right on it.

June 10: Wife requests definition of phrase "get right on it." I explain to wife that summer has been exceptionally hot and attempt to point out to her the futility of painting in hot weather.

August 18: Upon somewhat unreasonable prodding by wife, I go to the outdoor shed to check painting equipment. Find two paint brushes stuck together in bottom of can. Skillfully pry them apart and pour turpentine on them. Brushes slightly more stiff than garden rake.

November 10: Upon rechecking painting equipment, find that turpentine has already evaporated. Pour more turpentine on brushes. Brushes have loosened to the flexibility of whisk brooms. Notice that step ladder rung is broken and make mental note of same.

January 5 (10:00): Wife suggests we pick out color of paint. I attempt to show her the futility of painting in cold weather.

January 5 (10:01): Go to home building supply to pick up paint chart.

March 9: While performing annual car cleaning chores, find paint chart wadded up under car seat along with Phillips head screw driver needed March 8, a comb and 32 cents.

May 11: Under no small amount of duress from wife I return to building supply and purchase caulk gun, paint scraper and handy stirrer stick. Inform wife that work will begin once NBA playoffs are over.

July 4: Wife requests to know exact length of NBA season.

August 17 (11:00): Discuss with wife the futility of painting in dry weather.

August 17 (11:01): Locate caulk gun, scraper, handy stirrer stick and wadded up paint chart in trunk of car. Retrieve two brushes and slightly damaged step ladder from outdoor shed.

August 17 (11:02): Drive to building supply to purchase two new paint brushes.

August 17 (11:45): Wife decides that we will take entire Labor Day week off so that I will have ample time to paint house. I inquire about borrowing scaffolding. Wife reminds me that house is one-story.

August 18: Stepdaughters complain that we will be taking our week's vacation after they have returned to college. Wife informs them that we are taking off to paint house. Stepdaughters understandingly agree that we need time to ourselves. One requests to leave for college early.

August 31: I point out to wife that stepladder rung is in need of repair and that I will get right on it.

(Next page is missing, appearing to have been inexplicably jerked out of book)

September 3: Painting contractor estimates that he can paint house within two weeks. I offer him the handy stirrer stick.

Wife mentions that electric dryer is not working properly. I say that I will get right on it. Wife calls Sears.

Party Fever

I was almost trapped in the house the other night by a natural disaster. If you don't already have an escape plan for your home, you should get one. You can never tell when your wife may decide to have a party of some sort.

Once you get yourself an evacuation plan, you should practice exit drills and emergency procedures so the same thing doesn't happen to you. These procedures include "crawling low", "feeling doors for heat" and "getting out of Dodge."

The womenfolk in our house (which includes a considerable majority over me) decided to have a makeup party the other night. Something like this could consume your house before you know it. By the time you see the driveway filling up with carloads of women, it's too late.

You definitely need a plan. Mine was called "head for the hills." This is an OK plan, except you can only ride around a small town so long. Riding down to the old Liberty Drive-In, turning around and going back through the Four-Way parking lot got old fast. Besides, after lap number forty-two, I was getting some mighty strange looks from the washerette.

Then I remembered that I had stashed away a

couple of cans of potato sticks in my desk drawer for such emergencies as this. I put them there right after a Tupperware party (or was it a home furnishings party?) during which I almost starved to death. Food gets real scarce right before one of these parties, let me tell you.

Not that there's a lack of food at these festivities, it's just not there for you to eat. It's there for the party. You can tell for sure if there's going to be a party at your house soon if the supply of off-limits food builds up.

I should have known there was a party brewing at our house because Julie cooked brownies, but the smoke detector malfunctioned so I got no warning. I think someone took the battery out after it kept buzzing through every meal.

Anyway, knowing there was food in my desk, I decided to sneak back into the house, even though firemen will tell you this is a dangerous practice. It's here that the handy key to the rarely used front door hidden under the flower pot comes in handy, unless you want to spend much of the night in the car. You certainly don't want to go in through the living room any more than a missionary would want to wade through a herd of cannibals.

Once inside the house and safely seated under my desk with my potato sticks, I heard things no outsider has ever heard before. I felt like I was listening to the Masonic rites.

The makeup party had more or less split up into two groups of women. The under-thirty crowd was sitting up front, listening intently to what the beauty consultant was saying. The older bunch was sitting in the back at a table discussing three topics: 1. underarm deodorant 2. recipes 3. toilet bowl cleaners.

The beauty consultant was making up some young

gal who obviously didn't need to be made up. The real challenge obviously lay at the back table, but this was a makeup party, not a revival.

The consultant was applying all sorts of concoctions made up of aloe vera jell, honey, almonds, lemon, lime and caramel crunch. All this had made the gals at the back table so hungry that they had already eaten up most of the brownies and part of the makeup.

Everybody had to take a test. You got five points for wearing blue, five points for bringing a friend, minus ten points for washing your face with soap, ten points for knowing where women age first, two points for staying awake. I ended up with a minus ten, even after breaking even on the washing of the face, not having washed mine at all. I knew where men age first, but I wasn't so sure about women.

After awhile, the girls up front got a chill, and cut off the air conditioning. This lasted about five minutes until the back table was overcome with sudden flashes of heat and almost combusted spontaneously before they could get the air back on again.

Then everybody passed around different makeup products and tried them out. There was a toner and cleanser and refining lotion and moisturizer and elbow cream, relaxing foot balm, fingernail cream, eye cream, eye liner and wrinkle remover (this was a big hit on the back row.)

It was noted that some unlucky woman had once gotten her foot balm and eye cream confused and had relaxed her eyes so that they were permanently crossed.

About this time several of the back table members, alerted to my presence either by the crunching of potato sticks or the uncontrollable laughter, suggested that might be in the market for a large dose of vanishing cream. I took the hint and rode back downtown to replenish my supply of snacks for the upcoming bridge party. Or is that jewelry?

The Dating Game

Someone once said that a relationship is what happens between two people who are waiting for something better to come along. Well, evidently Sue Lynn found something better because she dumped Willard like a hot potato. Willard was not too pleased over the circumstances because he and Sue Lynn had dated on and off for several years and besides he had just shelled out over four dollars to take her to the local Opry house.

Probably the biggest mistake Willard had made, though, was in taking Sue Lynn to Biltmore Estates. Going somewhere like this sets a woman on fire and when she gets home and looks around at her meager furnishings, she thinks she's been robbed. A man can live quite well on a dirt floor, but a woman must have shag carpet.

On the way home, Sue Lynn had wanted to stop at Marlene's Mobile Homes and look at the new double-wides. Willard wanted to get home and check his trot-lines. An argument ensued and Sue Lynn had split.

"I don't understand women," Willard moaned. "They are so ungrateful. Here I spent the best years of my life with Sue Lynn and she throws me out over a chandelier.

Looks like a woman would be satisfied with a flashlight."

"The best years of your life?" I asked. "From 46 to 47? And nobody wants to eat supper by a flashlight, Willard. Women want romance."

I did feel sorry for Willard having to start all over again for the umpteenth time. I don't know how many of you have ever been single lately, but you reach a certain age where it becomes a drag. First of all, it's difficult to meet other single members of the opposite sex. Then when you do meet them, you've got to go through this introductory stage of "Well, what kind of music do you like?" or, in some cases, "What kind of denture cream do you use?"

But then Willard had been taken off wife support before and had managed to survive.

"Sandra and I can probably introduce you to some nice gal," I finally offered. "We can double date some weekend."

"Yeah, thanks," mumbled Willard. "I remember that last blind date ya'll got me. We met at Kidd's Drive-In and I watched her get out of the car. And get out of the car. And get out of the car. They had to put a board across two chairs so she could sit down."

I told Willard it was obvious that he hadn't looked in the mirror lately. Willard was of the belief that there was someone for everyone, but I figured Willard's someone lived in New Zealand. I did know, however, that we needed to find Willard a date quickly or he would be over at our house from dusk to dawn everyday.

"As many times as you've started over," Hoyle said, "you ought to have the hang of it by now."

"Well, it don't get any easier," Willard replied, propping his boots up on a piece of furniture. "Take my two marriages. The first one didn't last two years, but I learned from it."

"Yeah," I said, "you learned not to marry another lady wrestler."

"That," Willard groaned, "was no lady."

"And you learned not to let nobody, especially a woman, get you in one of them flying deadlock toe holds, too," noted Hoyle.

"Oh, I could have gotten out of that by myself," said Willard. "Ya'll didn't have to call the EMTs."

"But I'm talking about serious stuff," he continued, setting a Coke can down on my genuine solid pressed woodchip end table with walnut-like finish, leaving a white ring on it. "Things that hold a marriage together. Matrimonial glue."

"When did you find this nuptial cement?" I asked him. "After the first marriage or the second?"

"It's all a learned process," said Willard. "After the first marriage, I didn't think I'd ever look at another woman again. Then my eyes healed up. But you learn basic truths over the years."

"Yeah," Hoyle agreed, "never marry a woman twice your size."

"And never go to South of the Border on your honeymoon," I offered.

"Well, I happen to like Pedro," said Willard, his feelings evidently hurt. "I can't help Bertha didn't share my interests. You have to marry someone who shares your interests. She wanted to go to Carolina Beach and hunt for shark's teeth. That ain't no fun. I thought Sue Lynn and I were on the same wave length, but when she wanted to buy that new trailer I could see she was too highfalutin for me. Now I'm all alone, again."

"I've got an idea," I told Willard. "The Greensboro News *and* Record has a "Personals" section.Surely we can find someone for you there." Willard didn't seem too enthusiastic, but I got the paper anyway.

"Now, here's one right here," I said. " 'Petite single white female, 45 years young, enjoys reading, dancing, quiet romantic walks. No smoking, no pets.' "

"Too demanding," said Willard. "Don't like smoking or pets."

"But you don't smoke," I protested.

"Yeah, but I might want to start," he said. "I don't want anybody holding down my ambitions."

"OK," I continued, "here's another one: 'Looks like Julia Roberts.' " Willard perked up.

"Oh, I'm sorry," I retracted, "it says 'Cooks like Julia Roberts.' But how about this one: 'Single, white female, 31, independent, honest, enjoys movies, beach walks and the simple things in life. Seeking honest, trustworthy, emotionally stable...' "

"Hey, that was close," said Willard, "until you came to that emotionally stable part. Women just expect too much. Read me another one."

" 'Divorced, white female, 46, desires single or divorced white male, 36-55, 5' 11" or taller, for serious relationship. Must like to laugh, be pleasing to the eye and up to taming this lioness...' "

"I've tamed my last lioness," said Willard, showing me his scars."Besides, I don't like the tone of that 'must be pleasing to the eye.' "

"All right," I said, "what about this one: 'Single white female, 29 and built like the Queen of Sheba, with substantial inheritance, seeks over-the-hill 47 year old who enjoys coon hunting, fishing, watching NASCAR races on

TV, shopping at Wal-mart on Saturday nights or just lounging around while I wait on his every need. Must have beer gut and look like he has been rode hard and put up wet. Would be nice if he didn't shave on weekends. OK to put feet on table or track mud into the house as long as he lets me wash and iron his clothes.' "

"Yeah," said Willard, "that's all well and good. But can she cook?"

My Mind is in the Gutter

The autumn leaves were beginning to fall, clogging up our gutters, and I was forced to buy an extension ladder so I could climb up to them and clean them out.

Walter Foster and I have been working on an invention for years now that will keep leaves out of gutters or empty leaves easily from them. Our dream is a device much like a garage door opener which, when you push a button, will tilt the gutters, dumping their contents on your head. So far, we have gotten to the stage where our invention consists of several sticks of dynamite inserted into the gutters and a process in which we light them and run like heck.

You can buy these screens to fit over your gutters with hinges that you can lift up to clean all the leaves that sneak in under them. These screens do seem to hold smaller leaves and twigs in the gutters very well, so that in several years they will compost just fine. Other than that, I can see no use for them.

Anyway, I had to go buy a ladder because Walter borrowed the one I had borrowed from him and never brought it back. I thought about calling him but I figured he might remember other stuff I had borrowed from him, so I decided not to push my luck.

So I bought a 20-foot extension ladder from Leon Routh at Liberty Hardware and Leon even loaned me his truck to haul it home. And, yes, I did eventually return Leon's truck.

The ladder was exactly like the one I'd borrowed from Walter, except that it had all its parts and it had all these little warning stickers all over it.

The labels said that I had purchased a 20-foot ladder, but the maximum working length was 17 feet and the highest standing level was 13 feet , one inch. My ladder was getting shorter and shorter. There was even a rung with a sticker on it warning not to stand there or higher. To do so would result in death and/or dismemberment.

"Warning, failure to follow all instructions may result in serious injury," one label read. "You must wear shoes with a tread. You should keep your belt buckle centered on the ladder at all times. You should keep the ladder clean and not store anything on it. You must destroy a ladder which has been damaged by fire or chemicals. You should watch for wires because this ladder conducts electricity."

"Never abuse a ladder," another sticker said. It even gave a ladder abuse hot-line to report any such mistreatment.

But the clincher was on the next label: "You should never use a ladder if you are not in good physical condition."

I put the ladder in the storage building on top of every Christmas decoration known to the free world and went back into the house.

"Did you get the leaves cleaned out?" Sandra asked. "And is that Leon Routh's truck in the driveway?"

"I haven't had time to clean any leaves," I explained.

"I haven't finished reading all the warnings on the ladder. Besides, I've got to put on a belt and my shoes are slick. Plus, I'm out of shape and have been for quite some time and have no business trying to clean out leaves in this condition."

I picked up the phone and dialed the toll-free number. A lady named Maria who was evidently hired for her command of the Spanish language answered the phone.

The warnings, she explained, were placed on the ladder to protect the consumer from needless injury and the company from expensive lawsuits. And, she added, the government agency OSHA (an acronym standing for Office of Strangulation, Harassment and Aggravation) had made them do it.

I asked her if she thought an out-of-shape person who was about a gallon of ice cream short of 200 pounds and sort of wobbly should even think about climbing her ladder.

She assured me that if I followed all instructions, read all the warnings and heeded all the advertisements, that I would have no time to be climbing any ladder.

Walter and I are going to have one warning on our new improved gutter cleaner: "Light fuse and run like heck."

The Line Forms at the Rear

I was waiting in line at the grocery store the other day when I looked back and spotted Peggy Stanford in line about an hour and a half behind me. This was an odd position for Peg to be in because it's very seldom that anyone is behind me in line. Usually I am King of the Line, a position also referred to as "pulling up the rear."

While waiting in line that day, I became close personal friends with all the other waitees. It occurred to me that I could write some on this book while waiting, but I had forgotten my typewriter. So I just balanced my checkbook while ensconced in line.

Waiting in line is the great equalizer. It's something we all have in common. There are a few ...presidents, vacuum cleaner salesmen and such...who can pay others to wait in line for them, but usually sooner or later, we are all caught in line.

The average person spends eight hours a day working, eight hours a day sleeping (more on Sunday) and the rest of the time waiting in line.

You wait in line at the grocery story, bank, post office, to eat out, to pay after you've eaten out, to go to the bathroom after you've paid to eat out and in traffic going home. The first thing we learn in school is how to wait in line.

We wait in line at funeral homes, to buy gas and to go to the movies. We wait in line to buy stuff at the mall, then wait in line to exchange it. We wait in line (sort of an un-line) in the doctor's office, which he calls a waiting room.

Waiting in traffic is Everyman's line and no one escapes it. Drivers who would run over their mother if she didn't speed up will slow to a crawl to watch a guy change a tire.

At amusement parks we wait in line in what appears to be an endless maze of cattle pens for upwards of half an hour for a 30-second ride. Then you can wait in another line for half an hour to pay $2.00 for 30-cents worth of drink.

Many restaurants have taken up the cattle pen approach, while others give you a number and others just take your name. A line by any other name is still a line.

If you served in the Armed Forces you know lines intimately. Many of us swore that we would never again wait in another line after we were discharged. Since then, many have starved to death while others are, at this very moment waiting in line, eating their words.

Businesses have done extensive research on waiting in line and have found that most consumers will allow moss to grow on their northern sides before getting out of a slow line.

I have a theory which I like to call, appropriately, "the line theory". This states that whatever line I'm in will be the longest line. Usually it works something like this:

I'm in line at the grocery store, a long line with lots of full carts and kids stepping on my toes. A cashier opens a new line and I and a little old lady with a jar of pickles make a run for it at the same time. The little old lady, being slightly more agile and by elbowing me viciously, gets in front of me. Still, I laugh confidently at the poor souls in the long line I just vacated, knowing that I have gone from 52nd in line to second.

The little old lady, however, has picked up the only jar of pickles in the entire civilized world without a price or even a bar code. The cashier calls a clerk from his break in Bogota to go look for the price. The clerk acts as if he has been called away from his mother's funeral and he and the cashier discuss their dissatisfaction with their jobs, their lives and people in general.

Finally the clerk finds the price, but the little old lady decides she needs dill pickles instead of sweet. The clerk retrieves these from the dill pickle farm, but gets the wrong brand. The lady has now realized that she has forgotten her pocketbook and goes to her car to get it by way of Brazil. On the way, she sees fifty-two long lost relatives, all of whom she has to talk to for long periods of time. Finally she finds her checkbook, but not her driver's license. She thinks the cashier has charged her too much and she knows she has a coupon somewhere in her purse. She wants paper instead of plastic and the bagboy has to go to Des Moines Paper and Pulp to get it.

All the while the waitees in the other line are marching out of the store, including Peggy, triumphantly waving their receipts in my face as they go. The manager and I leave the store together as he cuts off the lights.

Working Three Shifts

Someone left a book on my desk one day not long ago. Since Sandra was the only other person home that day, I suspected her.

The book was *Second Shift* (Viking Books) by Arlie Hochschild and after scanning over it briefly, I realized I was entering foreign territory. Hochschild has given the name "Second Shift" to that domestic duty disproportionately borne by working mothers after the paid work of the day is done.

Hochschild did some research and found that about 20% of couples shared domestic work equally. Of the remaining 80%, about 70% of the fathers did around a third of the work and 10% did less than a third, usually next to nothing.

I don't know where most North Carolina men would fall in this survey. On their faces, probably. George Gobel, a man close to my own heart, said that hard work never killed anybody. He went on to say that resting is responsible for very few casualties, either. Hochschild contends that not only is resting hazardous to your health, it also causes quite a few divorces.

Personally, I'm pretty good around the house. I find

it hard to do nothing for long periods of time because I can't stop and rest occasionally. I mow the yard and take out the garbage. If I spill something, I will wipe it up, usually in the same day. I'm not so rude that I won't move my feet when Sandra's sweeping under them. In case of national emergency, at which time all restaurants would close, I can make a sandwich. Sometimes I grill a streak or a few hamburgers and usually end up burning them.

All this, of course, disproves the theory that men are helpless around the house. If trained properly, most men would be quite capable of performing most common household chores.

Men will tell you privately that Saturday morning golf is really a drudgery and how few women understand the sacrifices made on the golf course. Most men, I think, would appreciate the break in routine a little housework would give them.

But Hochschild claims in her book that the majority of wives have tried to get their husbands to help with chores and that most had given up. They decided that it was easier to do it themselves or that they were better at it than men.

So, here lies the answer to the problem. Men need to be better educated in the area of household chores. We have the need to break the monotony of our dull lives. I have to believe that most of us can be domesticated and that most of us can do anything a woman can do around the house, except perhaps cleaning grout. I have no idea where Sandra even keeps the grout.

Anyway, all we husbands need is an education. So, I propose a new course of study in local community colleges: Household Chores. This program could lead to either a two-year or a four-year degree. I could even teach a few courses, having received the third degree in this line of work many times.

Men majoring in Household Chores would have to start out with classes on how to raise children. This, according to Hochschild, is one of the major responsibilities men shy away from. Surveys have indicated that most men can recognize their kids in a crowd. I guess a good place to start in this course would be to get the men to memorize their children's names, then go from there.

The next part of the curriculum could be cooking. This would include turning on the stove and common areas of the kitchen where the stove might be located. It could include tips such as not placing tinfoil in the microwave and differences between bake and broil. This section would also include dishwashing and probably would result in many men coming home from class with brand new electric dishwashers.

Washing clothes would also have to be covered, since most men don't know whether they're washing or hanging out most of the time. Students would learn how not to mix dark clothes with light clothes and what to do with grey clothes. They would also learn the basic chemical reaction that causes a red towel to fade and turn your underwear pink.

Courses on various types of cleaning would take up several semesters. But this shouldn't be too difficult a course of study judging by many of the commercials that air during afternoon soap operas. According to these, you just spray some stuff on your walls and lounge around the pool while it washes, disinfects and deodorizes every room in the house. If you buy the right cleaner, it even has little brushes that run around under their own power and scrub your tub for you while you snooze.

A good thing to remember here is not to use oven cleaner to clean your hubcaps unless you can heat them to superhot temperatures. Not even the wife's good towel will take this stuff off.

There would be special instruction on mysteries like ironing. After several weeks of classes in this, a great number of students would come home armed with new permanent press clothes and the dry cleaning industry would undergo a boom period.

Community colleges would also set up special interest courses on how to wipe your feet and picking up after yourself. And there's dusting, window washing and diaper changing. The possibilities are endless...to bleach or not to bleach. To mop or sweep. Hot water or cold. Windex or Gas-Ex.

And all over the country, every night of the week, you could hear guys saying "Sorry, honey, I can't help with the chores, tonight. I'm late for class."

Deer Me

Okay, I watched the movie B*ambi* and, yes, I cried when the momma died in the fire. And I have been heard in the past to say "how could anyone shoot such a lovely creature with those big brown eyes?"

And I'll admit that they're pretty to watch as they eat every bloom in your pea patch or completely wipe out your canteloupe crop. And they're graceful and quick and leap a fence like it isn't even there. And the fawns are cute and the bucks are majestic.

But, I'll be dad-gum (pardon me if I cuss) if the cussed things aren't about to take over the state of North Carolina.

It's getting so that it's hard to hit a possum for the deer in the road.

In case you're wondering, I hit a deer the other night, or I should say, a deer hit me. We were riding over to Chapel Hill through the country (deer alley) to watch the mighty Tar Heel basketball team whip up on the lowly Rainbows of Hawaii. I have such considerable influence at Carolina that I am able to get tickets to such games as this and usually also get to see the Heels play Butler, Marshall and Russia.

I took Willard to this game because the last time I

took Sandra, she pulled for the Russians. It's highly embarrassing when your spouse stands up and yells "Go Reds!" in front of (or I should say "in back of") 21,000 Carolina fans. I said "in back of" because there are very few fans sitting behind us. We are up in an area where oxygen masks pop out of the ceiling in case of emergency.

Anyhow, here were Willard and I riding along minding our own business, when out of the darkness appeared a devious, car-butting deer. It headed right for the front of the Jeep and I immediately knew that it intended to leap through the windshield, hoove us to death, and then run for safety. I managed to turn the Jeep slightly, so that the deer only head-butted the front turn signal, spun into the passenger door and flipped off into the darkness again.

Stopping the Jeep, I got out to survey the damage. Willard didn't get out because (1) His door was permanently welded shut (2) His pants were wet. I found no sign of the deer except for the several thousand dollars damage it left.

To make things worse, we got to the game and Willard cheered for the Rainbows. "They're underdogs," he said.

Heck, so was that dumb deer.

You know, it's time the State of North Carolina realized we've got us a crisis situation here. I can foresee having "deer advisories" on T.V. in a couple of years.

"Motorists are advised to stay off the roads tonight because of huge drifts of deer all across North Carolina. The Highway Patrol has warned that the roads are clogged at this time. The Department of Transportation is working overtime to clear the roads, but it may be morning before..."

So far, the State seems to have a two-pronged policy toward the deer problem:

1. To erect signs at all deer crossings, so that deer may cross the road safely.

2. To create an extremely short deer hunting season with laws designed to make the average deer hunter look like an idiot.

Can you image a deer looking for a crossing sign so he can cross the road? What good are these signs? Does the State actually think these are the only places deer cross? And, if you slow down at these signs, this only gives the deer a better chance to jump onto your car.

You may be interested to know that the deer harvest in North Carolina generally runs around 118,000 annually. We have been using the word "harvest" for quite some time now because it sounds a lot more sanitary to say "Lawrence and I harvested three deer yesterday" than "Me and Larry blew three deer away last night." The word "harvest" brings a vision of wheat and corn instead of blood and guts.

I figure if 118,000 deer were harvested by hunters, then another 300,000 are killed off, er, harvested, by poachers and at least 500,000 are run over in the road. Probably about 500 die of natural causes, such as canteloupe indigestion. This leaves, according to my figures, only about ten million deer left in North Carolina.

The Wildlife Commission tends to disagree and estimates the deer population in North Carolina to be only about 800,000. Why they don't call it the "deer crop" is beyond me, but I think the figure is a tad low. 800,000 might be right for the Piedmont, but what about the rest of the state? Somebody's been fertilizing this crop, let me tell you.

With this many deer in the state, it's hard to walk in the woods without stepping on one. So why is it that the average deer hunter never sees one during hunting season? Where do they go? Montana?

Every year thousands of hunters continue an ancient tradition first begun by Indians in days long gone by, that of laying out of work to go deer hunting. The early Southern Indian tribes first hunted the white tail deer in North Carolina with spear and bow and arrow. They smoked large amounts of meat for later use. Deer probably provided 50 to 80 percent of their protein.

Today deer provide 50 to 80 percent of all the lies told at local stores and restaurants.

Around here, the question asked is not "did you kill a deer?" it's "have you seen any deer?"

That's usually answered by "Well, I shot at something that looked like a deer. Is dog season in yet? I sure hope so."

And this so-called deer, particularly if it got away, grows bigger and bigger every year. The first year, there might have been some doubt as to its sex. After awhile, it has a rack the size of a rocking chair. Given time, it may even become a moose.

When deer season opens, nothing brown and warm in the woods is safe from being shot at and missed. Every now and then a farmer has a cow killed by deer hunters and some even paint the word "cow" on theirs although it's a known fact that many deer hunters can't read.

Men will sit twenty feet up in a tree stand for hours in freezing rain with the wind chill down in the teens just to get the chance to kill something most of them can't even cook. But let their wives ask them to go down to the Food Lion to get a couple of steaks and its "Oh, honey, it looks like rain, and besides the Redskins are about ready to kick off. Couldn't you go?"

If deer were a foreign army, we'd be in enemy hands right now, in spite of all these camouflaged guys running around in the woods who won't see a deer until they're riding home that night. This is because our hunters' hands are tied by silly laws such as those banning the use of automatic weapons and hand grenades.

I urge the legislature to act immediately to make the deer season year round and to make it mandatory that each citizen over sixteen kill his quota of deer annually. Doe season should run from October to September. Deer hunting should be a required grade school course. The DOT should randomly move deer crossing signs periodically to confuse the deer. Spotlighting should be compulsory. Bambi should be banned.

I know the insurance companies would support this law. I called mine after the deceitful deer hit the Jeep and I heard her tell a co-worker "it's another deer." The body shops, on the other hand, will lobby against this idea. Deer have been as big a blessing to body shops as the BB gun has to the glass business. I stopped at a body shop to get an estimate and was told the guy who did "the big ones" was out that day. He was deer hunting. I was also told that I was their third deer victim that day.

The sad thing about it is that I will probably end up killing more deer than the body shop guy.

I think I've got this deer thing figured out though. I've purchased some deer whistles to go on the Jeep that will repel any deer with a thought of ambushing me.

They make the frightening sound of a deer hunter's teeth chattering in a tree stand.

Tubing

"Why don't you get everyone together and come up some weekend and we'll go tubing?" Jamie asked us one seemingly normal spring day when both Sandra and I appeared to be lucid but actually must have been in a zombie-like trance caused by wearing our socks too tight.

"OK," we both answered, having taken leave of our senses so long ago that we'd forgotten where we'd left them.

I don't remember exactly what I envisioned when Jamie said the word "tubing", but I think it involved scenes of White Lake from my childhood. Dad would blow up a couple of inner tubes and we'd float around the calm, crystal clear waters of White Lake until we were suitably sun burned, then we'd go home.

Sandra must have envisioned something even more serene, such as tanned, muscular attendants wading out in these calm, clear (did I mention warm?) waters to serve her cold drinks and crackers.

She immediately began calling all our friends, who in turn began planning a grand tubing expedition. Most were excited about the shopping opportunities which abound in the mountains and had thoughts of gathering a trunk full of crafts after a relaxing afternoon of tubing.

Some of our friends, like Walter or Big Ed or Erik, aren't adverse to adventures such as this. Others, like Susan and Peggy and Sandra may have accidentally stepped in mud before, but let's just say none of it got between their toes.

Let me explain that at the time Jamie attended Western Carolina University in Cullowhee. There are two frontiers left in America these days: Outer space and Cullowhee. To get to Cullowhee, you just go to the Great Wall of China and take a left. But even though Cullowhee is nestled far in the mountains of North Carolina and is nearer to Alabama than it is to us, there was no reason for us to believe that a tubing trip there would be any-thing but a lark.

One reason we did not fear a tubing trip is that Jamie, a ninety-pound bundle of energy, light and laugh-ter, never realized that we had a back yard when she lived at home. The only time her toes touched dirt was on the way to the car. Her idea of the Great Outdoors was a day at the park under the pavilion. If she suggested a tubing trip in the mountains, it must be safe, secure and antiseptic, we surmised.

It's not that we're not adventurous, mind you. We'll go shopping at the drop of a hat. Most of us tend to shy away from things that have the potential to break bones, like sky diving, hang gliding and white water rafting, how-ever.

The closer the day for the tubing trip creeped up on us, the more enlightened we became about tubing. We got this enlightening bit by bit.

"Don't worry, Momma," Jamie said one day right out of the blue while we were eating supper. "They make you wear life jackets when you go tubing. It's a law."

"What do you mean 'life jackets'?" Sandra asked. We both knew we never wore life jackets at White Lake. Besides, you couldn't very well eat crackers and drink cold drinks burdened by a life jacket. And a life jacket would certainly make you tan unevenly.

"So you won't drown if you knock yourself out on a rock," Jamie answered logically.

"Rock?" asked Sandra.

"Well, not just one rock," said Jamie. "Rocks. There are lots of rocks in the river, mostly where the rapids are."

"Rapids?"

This conversation went on like this right up to the day the twelve of us reached the river. By this time, Jamie had divulged most of the information concerning tubing, including the part about the snakes. This is when I thought we would lose half the contingent, but evidently years of shopping had hardened them to anything.

Susan was concerned about messing up her hair, which by the way looks a lot like a Fuller Brush. No one on the trip had ever seen her hair messed up and the thought of this gave us something to look forward to.

The staff at the tubing site took our minds off hair, though. They made us each sign a release form that basically absolved them from any responsibility for our death, drowning, dismemberment, disappearance or divorce.

They also provided us with huge tractor tire tubes, some of which had boards across them as seats. They did not have enough with seats, however, so we men took the seatless ones on the assumption that if God had meant for tubes to have seats, He would have made them bucket seats.

Then they crammed us into a van for the short trip up the river. Packed inside the van, life jacket to life jacket, I surveyed the faces of my friends, some of them more pale than others. It reminded me of the 82nd Airborne enroute to their D-Day jump over Normandy. It occurred to me at this time to mention the leaches.

There's something about the peer pressure of a group that holds it together, even in the time before they are certain to become leach bait. It does not deter them, however, from flailing the living daylights out of the bearer of the bad tidings.

We managed to turn a two hour tubing trip into a three hour trip. The water was cold, but your body has a way of compensating for this by turning absolutely numb, except for the feet and calves which stayed cramped most of the time.

The spot on the river which we embarked from had a small island in the center of it. The current pulled the women folk past one side of the island and the men folk along the other side. The women, afraid that they were traveling down a different river than we, began to scream for the Coast Guard. I knew when Susan began to holler for her hair dresser that we were in for a long trip.

Once we were reunited on the other side of the island, we began to practice our tubing skills. We found that if you flail about wildly with your arms and legs, paddle and back stroke for your life, eventually your tube will go exactly the opposite of where you want it to go.

The tubing people had warned us not to get out of our tubes for any reason. They emphasized this by telling us that our feet would get entangled in debris and that we would surely drown.

Sandra and Susan immediately got hung up on the

very first rock they spotted, one about the size of Mount Rushmore. Both were in about three inches of water, but neither would leave their tube, envisioning man eating trip wires just beneath the surface of the river waiting to ensnare them. Sandra continued this trend for several more rocks, until friendly canoers finally freed her. She was so grateful that she decided to ride in tow with them the rest of the way until Jamie pried her white knuckles from their canoe.

Walter and Susan kept floating over to the bank, a place of calm waters where many limbs hung over the river. They opted for the rapids, however, as soon as they found that many of the "limbs" were moving. I would have given up my tube and a hot shower to have seen a snake drop into Susan's lap, but there were no snakes that brave.

After my bottom had hit every rock between Dillsboro and Cherokee, I realized why the boards across the tubes were such a good idea. Jamie, on the other hand, was floating around like a little water bug. I guessed that she hadn't let college interfere with her education while at Western. Ed and Peggy found the trip "serene", causing me to wonder what mind enhancing drug they had taken before breakfast.

We all eventually made it back to the tubing place looking like drowned wharf rats. The guys were actually surprised to see us, I think, and were just fixing to launch a rescue party before it got dark. Susan, of course, looked like she just came out of Madame Pompadour's.

Next time I guess we'll go for the white water rafting. Either that or the shopping.

All That Glitters is Not Tinfoil

One Sunday Sandra and I watched in the park as two men walked over the grounds with metal detectors. Every now and then you'd hear a beep and one of the men would bend over and poke around in the dirt awhile.

I told Sandra I wished I had invested in a couple of rolls of pennies and could have scattered them around before they got to the park. It would have made their day.

Sandra seemed to think that was mean, but I convinced her that they weren't out there to get rich, just to have some fun. I assured her that if they wanted to get rich, they would never have purchased metal detectors.

Willard and I learned this lesson the hard way. Willard had bought one of these advanced metal detectors that filtered out things like hard cash, jewelry and platinum and went straight for pop tops and plow points, especially if they were buried knee deep in hard clay. I opted for a cheap metal detector that didn't discriminate against anything.

Willard had talked me into this treasure hunting thing. He'd read in some magazine that many people actually make quite a good living poking around with a metal detector and a garden trowel.

He showed me one headline in his magazine that read: "Man Makes Living With Metal Detector." It seems that some fellow quit his job with IBM because he was finding so many watches, rings and solid bars of gold on old church picnic sites that he didn't have room to store them and had no need to work for a living anymore. This same guy and others were selling, for a nominal fee, their secrets of success along with genuine maps of locations of buried treasure and probably real estate in Florida, too.

I tried to convince Willard that if the authors of these books knew where this treasure was, they would go find it themselves. This puzzled him for awhile, until he decided that these writers were either too rich to dig around looking for gold anymore or that they were just trying to help out those of us less fortunate, novice treasure hunters.

So Willard ordered these books and this high powered metal detector and we set about to learn how to get rich quick. I noticed right off the bat that the so-called maps of buried treasure were not quite as specific as they should be. For instance, the map of North Carolina had an "X" near the border of Chatham and Alamance Counties which, to me at least, didn't really pinpoint any gold doubloons with any great certainty since it covered a ten-mile area.

This was all Willard needed, however, to set him on fire. He suggested we spend our next Saturday in Alamance County, figuring it would take, at best, half a day to find the loot.

I reminded him that we might not be the only treasure hunters to order this book, a thought which again left him slightly perplexed. I also pointed out that the "X" in question was almost the size of the city of Greensboro on the map, quite an area to cover on a Saturday morning.

None of this deterred him. This was the site of where Simon Dixon hid his gold on Cane Creek in what is now Snow Camp, N.C., he said, and we were going to find it. He was sure of it.

By the aforementioned Saturday, Willard had reached the intensity of a football player at the Super Bowl. He had spent all night reading his treasure books and he was so pepped up you'd have thought he'd been to one of Zig Ziglar's seminars. He'd read about treasure hunters tripping over Mason jars full of silver dollars while loitering around corn cribs. One man, according to the book, had been fishing and fell into Blackbeard's treasure chest while taking a leak. Another had been to Biscoe to a tractor pull and discovered a lost Inca village filled with silver ingots. Yet another had run into a suitcase full of Susan B. Anthony dollars while planting okra in his garden. The success stories just went on and on.

As we drove to Snow Camp, I told Willard I'd heard the legend of Simon Dixon's gold. Old Simon was my fifth great-grandfather and I'd heard the tales while growing up. Simon, a Quaker miller, had supposedly hid his gold from Lord Cornwallis' troops, who took over his house after the Battle of Guilford Courthouse. Cornwallis, upon hearing that Dixon had buried his gold, tortured him, according to legend. Dixon died of his injuries, but the gold was never found.

"Just a legend," I assured Willard. "Trust me, nobody in my family ever had any gold. Nobody in my family ever had two quarters to rub together. I remember carrying a sweet potato to school everyday when I was growing up. One day I decided to trade my bag with my brother cause his seemed to be bigger. I sneaked outside at lunch and hid behind a tree to open his sack. It had a hicker nut and a flint rock in it."

I could see Willard's spirits drop because this was pretty strong evidence against us ever finding anything in Snow Camp. But we went anyway.

The site of Simon Dixon's mill, at that time, was just a rock foundation and a dam with the remains of a mill run still visible. The spot where the old rock house stood was just a hole in the ground. Now a home sits on the site but at the time, it was mostly wooded.

I don't know if Willard's books mentioned the wisdom of treasure hunting in the summer or not, but I began to realize that the people finding the real treasure were the ones who sold the bug repellent, suntan lotion, calamine lotion and snakebite kits, none of which, I might add, we had in our possession at the time.

The snakes were our first problem. Living in the old mill pond for 225 years of undisturbed luxury had fattened them up and also made them a tad ill at unwanted visitors. It got to be a bit disconcerting when you had to push the snakes out of the way to walk. But the mosquitoes, who evidently hadn't eaten anything since they chewed on old Cornwallis, took our minds off the snakes.

I reminded Willard of the fiasco in Pennsylvania when we had the run-in with the Park Service merely because Willard decided to dig up the site of Pickett's Charge at Gettysburg.

"Do you even know whose land we're on?" I asked him.

Willard had the theory that the song "This Land is Your Land, This Land is My Land", was part of the Second Amendment to the Constitution.

It didn't matter because we didn't last long on the creek. We did manage to dig up quite a collection of tin foil, though, before the ticks frightened off the mosquitoes.

On the way back, Willard stopped at every ball park bleacher, schoolhouse, old abandoned home place covered with wisteria and various bogs, quagmires, marshes and everglade-like cattail filled swamp we came to. Each time, we'd scan the ground with our metal detectors, finding various valuable Vienna sausage cans, collectable jar lids and antique spent shotgun shells.

Once home, Willard seemed to think we had quite a lucrative trip.

"If you'd just told me sooner that Simon Dixon was in your family, you could've saved us a trip to Snow Camp," he said. "Ya'll might not have had two quarters to rub together, but you sure were the tin foil kings of the county."

All in all, in cash money, we found eleven cents. I found the dime. I told Willard that counting our time and gas, we could go in the hole if we made many more of these trips.

That's when I put my metal detector up for good. When I left Willard's, though, he was planning a beach trip. He'd read in one of his books that someone had found a wash tub full of jewelry on Myrtle Beach right after high tide.

I left him my dime and tinfoil collection to help with expenses.

Squirrel Wars

I have nothing against squirrels. Squirrels are OK if they're fixed right, like in a Brunswick stew. I wouldn't trade a T-bone for one, but if you're having a hard winter, a squirrel will do in a pinch.

So, when I saw the squirrel in my bird feeder, knee deep in sunflower seeds, it didn't bother me one bit. I just went to get my gun.

Having grown up in Chatham County, I had often hunted the gray squirrel with considerable luck. As a matter of fact, my memory of the luck grew more considerable with every year that passed. If the truth were known, we would have starved to death if left to me to bring home fresh meat in those days, but the truth is rarely known at my house.

Since those days of my youth, the gray squirrel, or Tre-Ratus Aggravatus as it is known in the scientific community, has overtaken the suburbs. So it wasn't a total surprise to see one in my backyard.

"Is this rusty thing in the attic my gun?" I asked Sandra.

"You can't shoot Mr. Squirrel," she answered sweetly.

The squirrel had been in my sunflower seeds less than an hour and it already had a surname.

"Besides," Sandra continued, "it's illegal to shoot a gun in the city limits. We've got houses within 30 feet all around us."

If I'd pushed my constitutional right to bear arms, I could have won this argument easily. But then who wanted to spend the night outside with Mr. Squirrel.

The sunflower seeds had been purchased in hope of attracting some wayward goldfinches to my feeders. So far I had managed to lure a horde of sparrows, two fat doves, several crows and what looked like a goldfinch but turned out to be a sparrow with jaundice.

Now the sunflower seed, which cost slightly more a pound than filet mignon, were being devoured by a hairy rodent.

There was only one thing to be done. When a man is deprived of his gun, he must fall back on the one thing that separates us from the animal kingdom: logic.

I drove down to the lawn and garden center.

"I'm looking for a bird feeder a squirrel can't get into," I told the clerk.

"There's no such thing," the clerk replied. "Don't you own a gun?"

"Of course I do," I said. "You don't think I'm a wimp or something do you? It's just that I've become more civilized over the years and don't need to shoot small helpless creatures in order to feel like a man anymore."

"In other words your wife won't let you," he said.

"Something like that," I replied, "plus, it's illegal where I live."

The clerk brought out a pad and pencil and pro-ceeded to draw a curious contraption consisting of a long wire, varying sized spools and baffles. In the middle hung a bird feeder.

"Hang this up," he said, "and your squirrel will never eat another sunflower seed."

I went home to build this wonderful invention. I found some clothesline wire in the shed, but needed some spools and baffles. These I found in the house, among stuff Sandra should have thrown away years ago. I took several spools of thread from her sewing cabinet and salvaged a bunch of old records, both 45s and 78s, for the baffles.

I strung all these on the wire, with the feeder in the center, and tied the wire securely between two maple trees. For good measure, I greased the wire with lard.

"I dare a squirrel to even attempt to get at those sunflower seeds," I told Sandra. "The Flying Wallendas couldn't traverse that wire."

"Well, the circus must be in town," Sandra said, "because there goes a squirrel on the wire now without a net."

I looked out the window and watched as a squirrel deftly leaped over five Fats Domino records and landed with a plop in the bird feeder.

"I hope those aren't my Fats Domino records," Sandra said, "they're irreplaceable."

There was a scream from the back yard. We rushed outside. There, underneath the maple trees, wrapped in wire and spools and broken records, was the meter reader.

"I hope these aren't Fats Domino records," he said, "they're irreplaceable."

I helped him up and brushed him off. There wasn't a squirrel in sight.

"That squirrel is so shook up he'll never return," I gloated. "This just goes to show that man can be victorious without resorting to violence," I told Sandra, ducking as she threw a handful of Fats Domino records at me.

From the other maple tree, a squirrel chuckled as he sat in the feeder chewing on sunflower seeds.

I grabbed a mop from the deck and raced toward the tree. Mr. Squirrel was so shocked he didn't move, but sat amid $4.50 worth of sunflower seeds stuffing himself.

I hurled the mop at him like a javelin. It flew halfway up the maple tree lodging there and frightening Mr. Squirrel so bad that he sat up and licked his paws. Probably greasy from all that sunflower oil, I surmised.

Taking off a shoe, I threw it right past Mr. Squirrel. It stuck in the dogwood tree behind him. I slung another one and lost track of it in the trees.

I picked up a garbage can lid and flung it at him like a Frisbee. It spun into the tree and fell clanking to the ground. Mr. Squirrel was so disoriented that he jumped down into the lid and sniffed around for some more sunflower seeds.

Finally I went into the house triumphantly.

"We won't have anymore squirrel problems," I announced.

"What's the lawn chair doing up in the maple tree?" Sandra asked. "And where in the world are your new shoes?"

"Look," said Jamie, "there are three Mr. Squirrels out there now."

"Four," said Sandra, "there's one in the lawn chair."

I looked out the window. It was a squirrel convention at the bird feeder. I ran back outside. This called for desperate measures, I thought, spotting the garden hose. I knew that squirrels were deathly afraid of water. Or was that cats?

I turned on the water full blast and adjusted the nozzle

to a stream that would have floored a cow. Aiming the hose into the tree, I sprayed squirrels left and right.

The water shot straight up into the tree and right back down on my head. The squirrels danced around on the upper limbs and showered me with water again. They were bound to be demoralized by the way they were jumping around in the water.

Through foggy glasses I noticed that all the squirrels had disappeared. Once again human ingenuity had triumphed over nature. Then I saw Jamie feeding 16 squirrels bread crumbs in the front yard.

I drove back to the lawn and garden center.

"You look like a drowned squirrel," the saleslady said.

"Thank you," I replied, "have some sunflower seeds."

"You need some new socks," she said noticing my shoeless feet. "That one has a hole in the heel."

"Never mind that," I said, "I need to know what I can do for squirrels."

"Feed them peanuts," she said, "they dearly love peanuts."

"Let me rephrase my question," I replied. "I need fewer squirrels. It's squirrel city at my house now and some even have names. Do you have any Squirrel-Be-Gone?"

She pulled a book from under the counter. It was an *Audubon Society Guide to Attracting and Feeding Birds Although for Millions of Years They Have Managed Quite Well On Their Own Until We Came Along.* She flipped to the page on Pests.

There are only three things you can do with squirrels," she read, "you can kill them, trap them or tolerate them. That leaves you only one rational alternative," she added.

"Kill them," I guessed.

She shook her head.

I drove home. Our yard looked like Water Country USA. Jamie was spraying squirrels with the garden hose. They were waiting in line for their turn. In the back yard "Going to Surf City gonna have some fun..." was blaring away from a hidden radio. Squirrels were sliding down the mop handle in the maple tree and landing in the puddles below.

Jamie handed me the hose.

"They seem to like it best when you spray them," she said. The squirrels sat up on their hind legs in the tree. I could have sworn some of them had on bathing suits, but the lawn chair blocked my vision.

"What's in the bag?" Jamie asked.

"Peanuts," I replied, "they dearly love peanuts."

Hear Today, Gone Tomorrow

It doesn't matter what kind of ailment you have, someone else has had it.

You can walk up to anybody on the street and say something like "I've had the worst case of leprosy lately. All my toes are eaten off..."

And they'll say "Oh, yeah, I had that back in '79. Eat off my whole arm."

Then they'll show you the stump. And they'll tell you how their Aunt Edith just disappeared one night.

"Leprosy eat her alive," they'll say.

And they'll tell you what doctors they went to, how long they stayed in the hospital, how much the bill was and how little the insurance paid.

I don't care if you found piranha in your bath water, half of North Carolina has, too.

"Them piranha has nibbled on my knees for years," they'll profess and then they'll show you the scars. "Had to start taking showers they got so bad."

I say this because of the time I had a bout with inner ear trouble. I'd never heard of but one or two people who had this problem before I came down with it. But just as soon as I contracted it, I found out that not only did most of the Piedmont have it, but that they all had cures for it.

One guy said his was caused by fluid on the ear and his doctor "just sucked it out." Another said antibiotics would cure it.

But most people just said "So and So has it and they told him all they could do was operate and then that might not work." Nobody ever seems to know who "they" is, though.

I started getting dizzy one day in December. Not being too stable anyway, I didn't notice it for awhile. I could never even ride the Scoobie-Doo roller coaster at Carowinds without getting sick, so I've been used to dizzy.

But this dizziness got worse and eventually culminated in a couple of deep-sea-fishing-drunk-like days when I couldn't stand up, lost my lunch and was in general pretty immobile. It reminded me of that fishing trip with Willard in that I was terrible sick and caught no fish.

I finally went to the doctor and explained that I had what seemed like fluid in my ears. It seemed that if I turned my head and hit it a couple of times, water should pour out. Of course, my head being basically empty, nothing actually ever came out of it.

The doctor suggested after two visits that I might want to see a specialist in what is called otology, a Greek word meaning "he who looks into your ear and shakes his head." So I went to this otology guy hoping, of course, that he wasn't the famous "they" in the "they said they'd have to operate."

While I was waiting to see him, I overheard him tell this little kid that he was going to run some kind of wire up his nose, but all the kid would have to do was breathe through his mouth. I was just getting up to leave, reconciling myself to a life of dizziness, when he came into my room.

He poked a light in my ear and made shadow puppets on the wall from the light that came through the other ear. Then he made me do several exercises I was already familiar with, having also done them for the Highway Patrol in my younger days.

I told him of the sensation of fluid on my right ear and showing great concern and finding that I had good insurance, he decided that I should have extensive tests to determine just what was wrong with this ear.

He turned me over to an audiologist (from the Greek, "stares at computer, shakes head") named Henry who, by the way, likes to drag race in his spare time.

Henry found that I had perfect hearing and good comprehension of most words except "wash, iron, vacuum and paint." He also checked my ear drum reflexes but not, thank goodness, with a hammer.

Next was my auditory brainstem response testing, in which Henry taped disks on my head and evaluated brain waves as my eyes tried to follow red dots.

I asked him if he'd ever had a patient who had no brain waves show up. He said only writers.

But Henry saved the best test for last, which involved him actually pouring cold water straight from the spring into my ears. The instructions for this test (probably straight from the Gestapo handbook) say that "the test usually causes no pain" which is mighty reassuring. The test is intended to make the patient (who by the way is there complaining of dizziness, but not complaining too loudly because "they" might operate) even dizzier.

Believe me if they pour cold water in Henry's ear just before the green light goes off, he can win every drag race he enters. Without the car.

It turned out that the freezing water test, otherwise known as the Himmler Maneuver, found my problem. Modern medical technology had found that I had "fluid on the ear." The test had actually narrowed it down, amazingly, to the right ear.

And, yes, I know all of you have had ice water poured down your ears before, so I don't want to hear about it, or your leprosy, either.

All I know is that my dizziness finally went away, as did the contents of my billfold.

Traveling Light

If there is one thing that both unites us and separates us as human beings it's our religion. It's not my policy to make light of anybody's religion because I know this is a personal choice, no matter how dumb it may seem to others. It is mainly my mission to report the facts and let you make up your mind to heap ridicule as you see fit.

With this in mind, I feel obligated to relate to you the story, as reported by the Associated Press, of the 20-member Hermandez family, whose name I have changed because of reasons that will soon become apparent to you. The Hermandez family, it seems, left Floydada, Texas one day in a Pontiac Grand Am bound for a religious retreat in Florida. You might note that a Grand Am is a mid-sized car, what with the way cars are being down-sized here lately. It is roomy enough, but it is no Trailways Bus.

Somewhere along the way from Texas to Florida, or perhaps before they left home, the Hermandez family clothes became possessed by the devil. I don't know exactly how ones clothes become possessed by the devil and it is not my habit to concoct or fabricate when details do not exist. I have occasionally heard people say "the devil made me do it." And from having served in the Army there, I knew long before Charlie Daniel's song that the devil inhabited Georgia (not to mention parts of South Carolina).

I have had my clothes act mighty strange at times, leading me now to wonder if perhaps they were possessed. My slacks have clung to my legs like homesick children at inopportune times, like job interviews and weddings. My pants have split in embarrassing public situations and my shirt tail will hang out like a flag blowing in the breeze when least expected.

Maybe this is what happened to the Hermandez family, but whatever did happen, it happened to all twenty at one time because they all decided to go to Florida stark naked.

At about the same time the devil became attached to their clothing, the Lord stepped in (according to a sworn statement by one of the Hermandez brothers) and told them to rid themselves of all their belongings, including wallets, identification and the license plate of their car. Conveniently for them, He allowed them to keep the Pontiac.

Now, if you've been to any of the beaches in Florida, you'll know that going naked is not frowned on in that state. But the area in between Florida and Texas is evidently another story.

So with twenty people in this Pontiac Grand Am, most likely sitting cheek to cheek so to speak, the Hermandez family set out for the Sunshine State. Now this is no short drive. I'm guessing it's well over 600 miles. I don't reckon it ever occurred to these twenty people that they might have to stop for gas or something to eat or at least get out and stretch and go to the restroom.

Personally, I would like to know their secret, not that I want to go around naked or anything. But anyone who can talk a family of twenty into going off on a 600-mile trip without any luggage, hair dryers, curling irons, thirteen changes of shoes and enough underwear to outfit the Air Force deserves some credit.

I can see me mentioning to Sandra, at the last minute before we leave for Myrtle Beach, that the Lord has told me that we should unburden ourselves of these twenty-some odd suitcases (some odder than others) and sally forth with a toothbrush and some underarm spray. I'd probably be seeing visions for quite some time afterwards.

Or can you see little Rolane on his first date explaining to his girl friend that he had a vision and having thrown all his money into the side ditch he won't be able to pay her way into the movie. However, he continues, the devil has also possessed his clothes and because of this he probably will have to go naked the rest of the night and would she like to go to the drive-in. This might give new meaning to the term "religious persecution."

Anyhow, here is the Hermandez clan cruising toward Florida, all twenty of them, and evidently the kids start singing the old religious hymn "99 Bottles of Beer on the Wall" or something similar, so whoever is in charge sticks them all in the trunk. This is one of the few sane things the family did all day.

In Vinton, Louisiana, the long arm of the law finally caught the whole bunch buck, er, red handed (or red faced). A deputy stopped the Pontiac and the driver got out only wearing a towel. Evidently, the Lord allowed him to keep this, the seats being quite hot, if you know what I mean.

Before the officer could say "Wilbur Mills", the Pontiac took off and after a short chase, butted into a tree. The twenty were carried to a local hospital where, in one of the few cases anyone could remember, they were asked to put their clothes on before being examined.

Later they were all turned over to a Baptist church awaiting relatives to arrive, which seems to be cruel and unusual punishment for only having gone naked.

FEMA to the Rescue

You may wonder how the federal government is able to leap, with a single bound, into rapid action in times of national, or widespread local, emergency. You have to look only back to Hurricane Andrew several years ago to find the prototype in handling national disasters. As a matter of fact, our government was so swift and thorough in their handling of what might have been the worst natural disaster in our history that most people in Florida knew within months where their homes were and most had found their children.

Such things don't just happen by accident. Years of preparation are always behind such endeavors. I can vouch for this having worked for the federal government in a couple of capacities (some of which were more voluntary than others) and always being under the pressure of knowing that I might be called into action at a month's notice.

I also have a close friend, Cletus Feemeister, who is a special agent with FEMA, the Federal Emergency Mismanagement Agency who is very familiar with the intricacies of government and who has added his expertise to this study.

FEMA (Feeble Emergency Management Agency) is the very agency which moved in and responded to Hurricane Hugo several years ago and is at this very moment still surveying damage in North and South Carolina. Of course, this very agency could still bound into action and help the victims of Hurricane Andrew.

According to Agent Feemeister and various news reports, it seems that events unfolded much like this in the days leading up to Hurricane Andrew:

Friday: Hurricane center in Miami reports a huge storm forming near the Bahamas, with winds approaching 200 mph. Immediately calls FEMA (Feudal Emergency Management Agency). The secretary at FEMA reports that it being Friday, all senior department personnel are engaged in high level staff meeting and do not have phones on their golf carts. Suggests Hurricane Center fax message.

Saturday: Hurricane Center has now named storm "Hurricane Andrew" and notes that it is nearly a category five hurricane, which is higher than a four but not nearly a six. A five, by the way, designates it as almost catastrophic and is as high as a hurricane is legally able to go, the Senate passing this bill during the gas shortage of 1974.

The Hurricane Center again calls FEMA (Futile Emergency Management Agency). Answering machine states that all personnel have gone home for the weekend and to call back Monday or leave message at sound of beep. Machine squeaks but never beeps.

Sunday: Special agent Feemeister of FEMA (Feculent...oh, well, you get the picture) who is attempting to find a ball game on TV, wanders onto a weather channel and perceptively spots news of Hurricane Andrew approaching the coast of Florida.

Feemeister grabs his Hurricane Emergency Kit and looks up definition of hurricane. "A cyclone of large extent," he reads, "usually with rain, thunder and lightning...rarely exceeding 100 mph..." Makes mental note to check into situation Monday.

Monday: Hurricane Andrew slams into the coast of Florida just south of Miami with winds of 160 mph. Feemeister hears reports of storm on radio while driving to work. Changes channel in attempt to find oldies and goldies.

After arriving at work, sends memo to immediate supervisor asking about action to take in case hurricane is serious. Supervisor memos back that Feemeister has used wrong form. Needs Form 189A, Questionnaire of Action Required. Feemeister, out of Form 189A, requisitions more from supply.

Supply, being temporarily out of Form 189A, 1992 issue (but having two million crates of the 1957 edition) requisitions more from Printing.

Tuesday: FEMA agents in the field report that citizens of Dade County are relaxing, many on couches, in the middle of the street. One agent is ordered to report to Homestead Air Force Base for a flight back to Washington. Phones in that he is unable to find Homestead Air Force Base. FEMA faxes him map of area. Another agent reports that area looks like a war zone.

Thursday: National Guard called out to Florida. Finds no war.

Friday: Special Agent Feemeister sent to Florida to assess damage and to offer assistance to hurricane devastated state. Sets up office in Atlanta, not wanting to be too near stench. Immediately informs press that either the state government of Florida or the Red Cross is in charge of recovery efforts, but that he will be getting back to them Monday. Today being Friday, he has important high level meeting of senior department personnel and can't be delayed because of early tee time.

Feemeister later wins special achievement award plus large cash bonus for efforts in aiding in the South Florida disaster.

Breathing Can Be Habit Forming

When I was growing up, smoking wasn't hazardous to your health, it was sinful. As soon as I found out it was sinful, I went out and bought myself a pack of cigarettes.

Mark Twain said he made it a rule never to smoke more than one cigar at a time. In twenty years of smoking, I smoked three or four packs of cigarettes, one at a time, everyday. Conservatively speaking, I smoked about 400,000 of these little tubes of tobacco, or about $10,000 worth of them.

Over the years I thought about quitting. I heard vague rumors of people who had quit and actually lived through the experience. Someone told me that a guy down the street had quit and as soon as he sobered up they would find out how he did it. I marked it off as a lost cause and made up my mind just to enjoy smoking down to the last puff.

When you've smoked this many cigarettes in your life, you have very few reasons, in your mind at least, to quit. You become socially, physically and mentally bound to them. Price doesn't matter. It makes no difference that the smoke irritates others. You shrug off health warnings with "you've got to die from something". The smell of smoke in your clothes, house and car doesn't matter to you because you can't smell it. The slight cough becomes second nature. You don't read anything bad about smoking because you've made up your mind it's not bad.

I was convinced that quitting smoking was impossible.

But then I quit. It wasn't the hardest thing I've ever done, but it ranks right up there with stepping off the plane in Vietnam. I had help, though, and if you're going to quit smoking, you definitely need help. Mine was nicotine gum. And my reason for quitting was simple. When I would go out to get the newspaper, I would be out of breath. Now, I've been out of money and out of gas, but one thing is for sure, I don't want to run out of breath. Not just yet.

You can quit smoking, too, and when you quit, or if you're thinking about quitting, here are a few things about it you should know:

1. Quit for yourself. This is very important because you'll find very little support once you've quit smoking. The same people who complained about your smoking will now complain about your aftershave or your haircut. So quit for yourself. Only you can get yourself through the really hard times.

2. Have a valid reason to quit. Mine was that I like to breathe. Every time I want a cigarette now, I take a deep breath instead. Sometimes I get dizzy from taking all those deep breaths.

3. Use a crutch if necessary. Mine was nicotine gum. It comes through prescription only and gets you through that two or three week period of physical withdrawal everyone dreads.

4. Once you quit, you may gain some weight. This is

like saying the mail volume might increase at Christmas. When I quit smoking my waist size was 32 and my life's ambition was to weigh 175. When I began gaining weight, I bought some size 34 pants, but outgrew them on the way home. Now I wear 36's and my ambition is to slim down to 175, a weight that I must've passed in my sleep.

Excessive eating, of course, is just one more habit to break. Food tastes better and eating can easily take the place of smoking if you let it. Start an exercise program. Watch your in-between-meal snacks. Be aware of the pitfalls of jumping from one bad habit to another.

5. Your sense of smell will return in style. In other words, you will be able to smell a goat burp in Cambodia. I never realized, for instance, that so many of my friends were hog farmers until I quit smoking. And the same people who complained about your smoking have bad breath.

6. Your legs will ache for awhile. I don't know why this is. Perhaps it's the blood returning to them after such a long absence.

7. Your breath won't smell like smoke anymore. It will smell like some strange combination of garlic and dirty socks. Buy some mouthwash.

8. You will save a considerable amount of money but will blow it on something equally as foolish.

9. You will gain some measure of freedom. You can leave the house without those three packs of cigarettes, matches and lighters. You can walk into a room without searching for ashtrays or smoking sections. You don't have to walk outside every few minutes to smoke.

10. You will live longer. But, as a friend said, who wants to live longer if you can't smoke?

As you can tell, I have mixed feelings about quitting smoking. One tends to remember the good times in any relationship and when you smoke three or four packs a day it's more than a relationship. It's a love affair. To quit smoking you have to adjust to changes in everything you do: eating, sleeping, drinking, working, associating with friends and being around other smokers.

On one hand, you give up the benefits of smoking that only confirmed smokers know—the social and emotionally satisfying aspects that help reduce nervousness and stress.

But on the other hand, you'll wake up feeling better. You won't cough. Your sense of taste and smell will improve dramatically and good food will taste better. Unfortunately, bad food will taste worse. And I've noticed that those balls I once couldn't get to on the tennis court...well, I still can't get to them, but I feel better trying. There are many other benefits but, in general, your overall health will improve.

Doctors, of course, will tell you all sorts of things about smoking...that it's the single most dangerous risk factor of heart attacks, lung cancer and emphysema. Of course, we all know this can't happen to us.

But the sad fact is that it can and does happen to us. If you can quit smoking, do it now. The first month will be extremely hard and even a year or two later you will find yourself wanting a cigarette. But suddenly one day you'll walk outside after a spring shower and realize how fond of breathing you've become.

Believe me, breathing is something you can grow accustomed to.

Burned on the Fourth of July

The Fourth of July always sends chill bumps up and down my spine. Not because I'm overly patriotic, mind you, but because that was the day Willard took one small step for man, one giant leap for mankind. Well, sort of.

You'd have to know Willard, I guess, and how much we wanted to climb the greasy pole and win that $20 bill that was nailed to the top of it. The Fourth of July was always flags and fun and hotdogs and fireworks, but mostly it was the greasy pole climb.

Much of the school year after Christmas which wasn't spent in dodging bullies like the Maynard brothers was dedicated to figuring out the greasy pole. In that summer of our childhood, Willard had finally come up with a way to climb the pole and win the money.

Some of you already know Willard. You might have seen him around town with his "Half Fast" cap on in the old car with the "Jimmy Crack Corn and I Don't Care" bumper sticker. He's the one who got Hoyle and me "the best tickets money could buy" at the Coca Cola 600 right down on the front row in the sun.

He's also the one who took Hoyle and me off Christmas Eve to buy last minute presents and ended up leading us through a swamp of blackberry briars looking for his coon dog. I've still got the scars to prove it. And then there was the time, earlier in our lives, when we went out with Willard to get a cup of coffee and ended up in Kentucky.

When we were growing up, Willard was the one Mom always said "wouldn't grow up to amount to anything." Sandra has changed that to "the one who wouldn't grow up." She likes Willard OK, she just feels that people our age should be mature enough to keep the Johnson grass from growing in the floorboard of their car.

Anyway, Willard has always been about the same, even when we were childhood buddies. Back then, the Fourth of July was a big deal. The town always had festivities with a parade of veterans and bands and floats, with games for the kids, fireworks and even a rodeo now and then. Speakers always lauded our forefathers and how they had fought and died for our freedom. And back then, we boys even took our caps off when the flag came by.

Sometimes we had our own fireworks. Usually an older cousin would drive to South of the Border and come back with enough fireworks to blow up the Hoover Dam. Even Johnny "Gums" McCaskill's accident didn't stop us from setting off fireworks. Johnny had been driving around town one Fourth, lighting fire crackers with his cigarette and throwing them out at us unsuspecting youngsters on the sidewalk until he threw his Camel at Millard Cook and took a long drag off a cherry bomb. Now, Johnny couldn't sneak up on anybody because you could hear his false teeth clicking like tap shoes for blocks away.

That one summer, Willard had come up with a masterful plan to finally conquer the greasy pole. We would dress up Little Hubie Perkins in jeans, long sleeve shirt and brogans. Then we would dunk him in the creek that ran beside the ballfield, roll him in the sand at the Monument Company across the street and then send him up the pole. The sand would give him enough traction to grab the $20 bill, which we would then split three ways and use to purchase as many Zero bars as we could safely carry.

We would enter the greasy pole contest ourselves and climb as far as we could before we sent Little Hubie in. We knew from experience that the first contestants were merely pole fodder and only helped clean the lard from the bottom part of the pole. The main thing we had to do, though, and which was no small task, was to keep the Maynard boys away from the pole long enough to get Little Hubie up it.

The Maynards had won the greasy pole contest for as long as we could remember, climbing it like alley cats. The Maynards always had that coal miner look about them, and we figured the accumulated grit of never bathing helped them in their climbing.

Plus, they were just plain mean, and meanness could get you a long way up the pole. They were so mean that they would wait in the school bus line behind us and poke nails in our back, demanding money. This was futile, of course, since we never had any money. I do hope, though, when the school board banned weapons on school grounds, they thought of nails.

When that fateful Fourth arrived, we approached the ballfield with visions of Zero bars dancing in our heads. Willard had scooped up a handful of cherry bombs from his cousin's trunk and put them in his back pocket to celebrate victory with later that night.

We had watered and sanded down Little Hubie, but judging from his slow, ponderous stride, I was beginning to have my doubts of ever getting him off the ground. Years later when I saw those first shots of Neil Armstrong walking on the moon, it reminded me of Little Hubie, except that Hubie didn't bounce.

At the greasy pole, things were not looking good. The younger Maynard boys had already cleaned off most of the lard off the bottom of the pole and were standing at its base, boldly puffing forbidden cigarettes while the older Maynard prepared to zip up it like a lineman for the county and grab that twenty dollars.

We quickly pushed Little Hubie through the crowd to the front of the line. Seeing some competition, the older Maynard shoved Little Hubie to the ground, where he looked like he was sure to lay till Autumn. I was about to shove the older Maynard back, an act I was sure would doom me forever. I knew that on subsequent Fourths, speakers would talk eloquently about the Alamo, Custer's Last Stand and That Poor Little Boy Who Shoved The Maynard Boy Out Of The Way.

But none of us had seen Mr. Maynard approaching until the father of these brats grabbed the oldest Maynard by the ear and dragged him off screaming.

We were all amazed at this occurrence because: 1) We didn't know they had a father 2) We didn't know they could cry. The younger Maynards were so shocked that they discarded their cigarettes immediately, one dropped in the sandy infield, the other stuffed in Willard's back pocket.

What happened next was a blur of events and all I really remember is a series of explosions which caused many of the World War II vets in attendance to hit the dirt. The next thing was completely amazing and Hubie and I discussed it at length over three pounds of Zero bars and an Orange Crush in the emergency room while waiting on Willard to be sutured up.

Willard had taken flight to the top of the pole, grabbed the $20 and slid quickly back down, smoking slightly from the area that used to be his back pocket.

Well, the band struck up "America the Beautiful" and the crowd erupted in applause. I did remember to grab the twenty from Willard's clammy hand as they hauled him off.

As Dad later said, the Fourth of July always reminded him of "the rocket's red glare, Willard bursting in air."

But to us the real meaning of the Fourth of July was reinforced, that being the American spirit of freedom and ingenuity triumphing over tyranny and injustice and leading directly to cash rewards.

A Fried Apple Pie a Day Keeps the Doc Away

Jamie came home from college one weekend warning us of the dangers of diet drinks. She said they caused irritability, memory loss and I forget what else.

I'll tell you what, that college is a good investment. If your kid hasn't gone to college, by all means send him as soon as possible. They come home that first weekend knowing more than Albert Einstein and they haven't even been to three classes.

So all weekend, Jamie was on a Diet Drink Patrol causing Sandra to quit drinking diet drinks, at least in front of Jamie. It took a lot of heat off me, though, since I don't drink diet drinks and I got to eat my fried potatoes for breakfast in peace.

I've never got caught up in this diet craze. When I die, I want to die from the Real Thing, not some substitute. I want all the caffeine, phosphoric acid and caramel color I'm entitled to.

Sandra is another story, though. She's hooked on diet drinks and when you mention to her that they may cause irritability she just gets irritated.

My weaknesses are most anything fried and, of course, ice cream. If you could fry it and keep it from melting long enough to eat it, I'd fry ice cream.

That night that Jamie was harassing Sandra, I left home with the sole purpose of buying some cherry vanilla ice cream to soothe my nerves. Butter pecan was my second choice and I was not adverse to settling for butter almond. As a matter of fact, I was willing to go as low as plain vanilla.

When I got to the store, the freezer was bare except for some chocolate and something called coffee ice cream, which I felt might keep me awake all night.

The stark reality of facing a night without ice cream sent my temper boiling and there's no telling where this would have led had I not been able to consume six or seven fudge sickles.

I thought nothing of this temper tantrum until I saw the paper the next day. Headlines read: "Cutting cholesterol may raise tempers".

Well, of course it could. It makes all the sense in the world to me. All of us have been faced with this surge of temper when having to settle for a broccoli casserole instead of big old juicy steak and a heavily buttered baked potato.

The paper said that researchers now feel that people on cholesterol reducing programs may be more prone to violence than those who remain on a more typical high fat diet.

I asked Jamie why she didn't know this.

"I've only been to school a week," she replied. "Classes haven't even started yet."

When you think about this, you might want to recall that many of our most recent wars have been fought with various rice-eating peoples who tended toward violence when shot at. And then there was that conflict in the middle of the desert with a people who live on camel yogurt and boiled palm fronds. No wonder everybody's so touchy. No cholesterol.

This research should revolutionize our way of thinking about fat, at least until new research comes out, which will probably be tomorrow.

Our schools first come to mind. There is a movement at this very moment to reduce the fat content of school lunches to 30 percent of calories consumed. Already some schools have NO deep fat fryers.

No wonder kids are taking guns to school and kids in California are wearing bullet-proof vests in class. We need to get these students some fried chicken and creamed potatoes and gravy fast.

Another result of this research will be the "not guilty by reason of low cholesterol" defense which will soon flood our courtrooms. This could also guarantee the continuation of my fried potatoes for breakfast, a tradition that the cook has threatened to end because "it isn't good for me."

Unfortunately, this trend won't last long. In this day and time we have researchers for everyone. Before Jamie leaves for college again, someone will say that diet drinks are OK. One researcher discovers that something is great for you, will cause you to live longer and get better gas mileage and the next one will come along and tell you it will slap dab kill you.

This is one reason I have formed a group called Cholesterolics Anonymous, which you can join with the donation of one or more fried apple pies. Our motto is to eat drink and be merry for tomorrow you may be beset by irritability, violence, loss of memory and I forget what else.

Antiques Ought To Be Old

I never thought you had to be antique to appreciate antiques. But antiques are getting younger. If you know what I mean.

It's like watching sports. The players keep getting younger and younger every year. I don't age, but those darn teams are staffed by babies nowadays.

Antiques are getting like that, too. Just the other day someone bought an unused 1964 Kellogg's Cocoa Krispies box for $795. Granted it had a full-color picture of Snagglepuss on it, but $795? And 1964 was just yesterday. The Cocoa Krispies were probably still crisp.

Antiques have always intrigued me, but they were old antiques. I would visit my grandparents and great-aunts and admire their corner cupboards and pie safes and pine chests and their thick pink glassware and their water dippers and buckets. It was always a dream world for me to be around so many antiques.

One day grandma set me straight.

"I grew up with this old stuff," she said. "Everyday of my life has been spent with this old stuff. I want new stuff."

And to punctuate her remarks, she later sold some

of her household furnishings to an antique dealer whose ad she'd seen in the local paper.

An antique dealer is someone who sells the same stuff you grew up with, for prices that, if you could have sold it for, you could have afforded something better.

I was shocked. She'd sold some quilts, an old table and who knows what else. But she explained it to me with perfect logic.

The quilts, she said, were shot. They were hand-made and the antique dealer was quite foolish to offer her $5 for the bunch. She knew a deal when she saw it.

And the table. The old table had sat on the back porch. Years ago someone had painted it purple and when storms came in from the south, the rain blew in on it. The dealer had offered Grandma $15 for it and she had jumped right straddle of this deal.

I told Grandma that if she wanted to sell her stuff, someone in the family would probably like to buy it. She didn't have to go to an antique dealer.

She let me know that no one in the family would have wanted that junk. Especially the table.

The table, she said, was really useless. It had been made by her grandfather, so the decrepit thing was probably a hundred years old. It was made out of walnut (she said "walnut" scornfully, like it was pressed wood) and didn't even have any nails in it, so I could imagine how rickety it was. It was put together with pegs, she scoffed.

I bid Grandma a quick goodbye and rushed over to the antique shop. The table was gone, refinished and sold. The dealer didn't remember who to, but it didn't matter. In 1964, I didn't have the $200 it would have taken to buy it. I went home and sulked.

I still keep an eye out, halfheartedly, for that old

table, knowing all the time I'll never find it.

Nowadays, Sandra and I roam around antique stores looking at, and occasionally buying, depression glass. Depression glass is so named because it sends you into a deep depression to see the prices on the same glass that service stations once gave away.

Awhile back we walked into an antique shop and something in the very back of the store caught my eye.

There across from an oak filing cabinet was the very model kitchen cabinet I had grown up with, complete with the built-in flour sifter and pull-out shelf. And beside it was the very scooter on which I had scooted down College Street in my youth, which I might add wasn't so long ago.

I had to laugh. Someone had really goofed when they put this stuff in an antique store. The cabinet sold for $145, the scooter for $30.

"Are you going to buy it?" Sandra asked when she saw me looking at it.

"Are you kidding?" I said. "I grew up with this stuff. I want new stuff.

I don't understand why they don't keep antiques old, like they used to.

Computer Illiterate

It's not that I've resisted change, it's just that I'm a conservative kind of guy and, well, I'm sort of slow, too. If it were left up to me, I'd write this in long hand with a lead pencil. But sometimes you need to get with the program and take a giant step into the Twentieth Century.

So, I bought a computer.

If I were you, before I died, I'd buy a computer. Nothing outside of getting married will make you feel so ignorant.

Let me say that this computer business was against my better judgment. Everybody told me how badly I need a computer. This should have made me skeptical from the start. Sometimes people talk you into something so that you can be as miserable as they are. But I trusted their judgment because they were people I admired.

At the computer store, the salesman's eyes lit up like a power surge protector gone bad when I told him I knew absolutely nothing about computers. I had tried to get Sandra and Julie to go with me since they are our family's resident experts on machinery, but all they said was "get some neat games."

Anyway, the salesman fixed me up and I do mean fixed me up. The federal government probably purchased less computer equipment last year and was more frugal in doing it. I noticed when I got home that I had a program on money management which, after buying this computer, will be totally useless for several years to come.

The salesman did mention to me, after learning that I knew more about space travel than computers, that I might want to take some computer classes at $80 a pop. I declined, confident that if I could master an electric typewriter in only five years, I could certainly master the computer.

The first thing I wanted to do once I got home (besides hide the sales receipt from Sandra) was to hook up the computer and start computing. I unpacked everything, the computer, the keyboard, the monitor, the mouse but left the printer in the box mainly because I had more paraphernalia than I knew what to do with.

Naturally I sought the handy User's Manual and found it among what seemed to be crates of books and strange looking disc-shaped things, which I stacked the books on top of.

I swear, I am not telling a lie, this is the very first thing the User's Manual said: "Jumper setting for the MB-4925D System Board. JP2: The CMOS Memory Board Reset Jumper. This jumper is used to clear the CMOS memory where the setup programs entries are stored".

I was afraid for awhile that I'd gotten some secret agent code book or something. Nowhere was there anything to tell me simply how to hook all these components to each other. Finally, it occurred to me that there was only one logical way to hook these things up. Each one was different and only went into one port. All of them, except the one I bent, which did finally fit nicely.

After this, things went steadily down hill. I did manage to put several programs into the computer that were already there to start with. I also learned that cussing a computer has absolutely no effect on it. Sandra also convinced me that hurling a computer has no useful purpose, either, other than to improve my disposition.

The printer was a great deal of fun. Sandra said she had no idea there were so many ways to say derogatory things about an inert object, and I do mean inert.

First, the instructions said to install the Image Drum Cartridge. After half an hour and Sandra intervening just in time to save the computer's life, it was determined that the Image Drum Cartridge had, in fact, been installed at the factory. Or by elves.

Then came the Toner Cartridge. I kept clumsily knocking off these fragile looking blue clips and carefully putting them back into the slots in the cartridge. After several times of nervously doing this, Sandra convinced me that it was necessary to remove these clips to install the said cartridge, as they were part of the packing.

You can't just hook up a printer and expect it to print. The computer has to accept the printer and there is a program for this. Mine said to insert disc number six to accomplish this feat. I did this, after finding disc six under so many books, which Sandra said would probably warp the disc, to which I said I was going to warp the whole mess before I was through. Disc number six did nothing but beep obnoxiously.

I finally called the computer store and got a technician who spoke English. After awhile, it was determined to try disc number seven, since the computer was probably playing with me because I had called it so many names. With this, the printer sprung to life.

So here I am, solidly in the twentieth century, except for my eight track, and typing this (or word processing it) on my computer, the one with several dents in the top.

I was never able to vent so many frustrations and try out so many new and varied cuss words with my typewriter. Ah, progress.

A Package Marked "Agile"

As many of you know, I work for the Postal Service, a job which allows me to meet various and sundry people, most of whom should be incarcerated. There was one day, though, that stood out from all the rest.

It was one of those days when nothing would go right. You know, the kind of day that makes you wish you'd gone into the service station business like Momma wanted you to.

Robert Frost said it best: "The brain is a wonderful organ; it starts working the moment you get up in the morning and doesn't stop until you get to the office."

He failed to mention that on Monday mornings, it rarely starts working at all.

I was in the back of the post office that Monday morning, trying to get the bits of Kleenex off my face, when the first customer walked in. I had chopped up my face shaving that morning. Kleenex will stop the worst bleeding known to medical science unless you've got your last clean shirt on. Then a tourniquet wouldn't stop it.

The customer had placed a shoe box on the counter.

"You think we ought to write 'this side up' on it?" he called out. "I'd hate for this stuff to spill."

I looked at the shoe box. It was a rather ordinary shoe box, except it had string tied around it and occasionally it moved.

"I want to mail it to Arizona," he continued.

"Did that box move?" I asked him uneasily.

"Yeah," he replied. "I sure hope they don't spill their water and pimento cheese. Maybe we'd better insure it, or at least write 'fragile' on it."

The conversation was going too fast for me.

"You can't mail this package," I told him politely. "It's not wrapped properly (I wasn't sure he was wrapped properly either, but didn't mention it).

"Besides," I added for good measure, "it moves."

"They'll move around some," he said knowledgeably, "but they can't get out. I'm sending them to my brother in Arizona for his birthday. He's never seen one."

I was beginning to wonder if I'd ever seen one and, if not, did I want to see one just now.

"Just what have you got in that box?" I asked. I explained that ordinarily I didn't have to know the contents of packages unless, of course, they moved.

"Possums," he replied proudly. "My brother's never seen one. I'm sending him three for his birthday."

I stood there for a minute thinking there must be a better way to start the morning than having to get up. Then I tried to explain to him that he couldn't mail a shoe box full of possums.

"They'll die," I said. "Your box isn't even ventilated..."

He untied the string and lifted the top off the box. Sure enough, there were three baby possums, a bowl of water and a pan of pimento cheese. They weren't exactly cuddly creatures, but were kind of cute.

"Do they really like pimento cheese?" I asked him,

stroking one of the possums on the head. It immediately clamped two rows of sharp teeth around my finger.

"They like meat better," he said as I held my finger. "But all I had was pimento cheese."

I searched for a Band-Aid. "Why don't you put some Kleenex on it like you've got on your face?" he asked helpfully.

The three possums had crawled out of the box and were snooping around the counter.

"I thought possums played dead," he marveled.

"They're not going to have to play if they're not out of here soon," I promised, holding my finger. I reached for the Domestic Mail Manual.

"Don't hit them with that," he pleaded. "You'll mash them."

I explained that I was just going to look up the kinds of animals he could send through the mail. I was confident that possums weren't one of them.

"Small, harmless, cold blooded animals, except snakes and turtles, which do not require food or water or attention during handling," I read, "and which do not create sanitary problems or obnoxious odors..."

One of the possums had created a sanitary problem on the money order machine, followed by an obnoxious odor. Another was chewing on the time cards.

I read faster. "Baby alligators and caymans not exceeding 20 inches in length, bloodworms, mealworms, chameleons, frogs, toads, goldfish, hellgrammites, newts, salamanders, leeches, lizards, snails and tadpoles are mailable..."

A scream erupted from the box lobby, where a customer had opened her post office box.

"I didn't order this thing and I'm not taking it," a

lady was yelling. "First it was those books and then the hosiery. But this is the last straw." I retrieved the possum from her box and went back to the manual.

"You can't mail these," I told the customer with the shoe box. "No warm blooded animals except day-old poultry are acceptable." I had finally found the reference.

"You mean I can't even mail them if I punch holes in the box and put some hamburger in with them?"

"You can't mail them with an air conditioner and T-bone steak," I replied. "Maybe your brother would like a newt..."

"I'll just mail him a shirt," he said, scooping the possums into his box.

"I'm sorry about your accident," he added.

I assured him my finger would be all right.

"I meant your face," he said as he walked out the door.

Southern Traditions

There is something quite mystical and mysterious that occurs when men get together with other men that causes them to act much like a horse's rear end. This is not to be confused with those confounding forces that compel men to act like horse's rear ends around women.

This phenomenon of men socializing with men is known as "male bonding", a term made up by psychologists for use on the Oprah Winfrey show. This male behavior is not related to "male bondage", which is a term used to describe the way males interact after marriage.

It is thought that the gathering of men in groups was first called male bonding because of the frequent bonds that were set at the local magistrate's office at the culmination of these fiascoes.

Male bonding is older than a jar of pickled eggs. It goes back to the beginning of human life to the Stone Age when men would gather to hunt and fish and to tell lies about both. The typical caveman who, by the way, looked much like a 300-pound tree trunk with ears, found it necessary to band together to hunt and protect their community and to set apart their masculinity from the female of the species who, by the way, looked much like a 300-pound tree trunk with ears.

It was around this time that cavemen realized that they could meet in their own private cave away from any undue influence from female minorities. By the time the wheel was invented, the average caveman was spending about three hours a week at home. This eventually resulted in the invention of the divorce.

Today, Southern men still feel the need to gather to tell lies, and although hunting and fishing are not necessary for survival, these two sports provide the best opportunities to do so.

It's difficult for many of our wives to understand the male psyche. Sandra, for instance, cannot see the reasoning behind going to a stock car race when it's being shown on TV. And, as hard to believe as it may be, she would rather sit and read a murder mystery than go frog gigging because "we already have food in the freezer and besides, I'm not going to eat 'em even if you do fry 'em."

There is just something abut the male need for adventure that defies logic, that goes deeper than slogging through the mud for a few frog legs and minor snake bites.

"There are," says my buddy Willard, "just some things a man has to do."

This need to bond and this desire for adventure has brought forth many Southern traditions: coon hunting, fox hunting, stock car racing.

There are some things that are just inherently Southern. Take hunkering, for instance. Hunkering is about as Southern as you can get.

There are not many people left now who can recall the golden days of hunkering. Not because they died, mind you, but because they abused their brains so badly in the '60's that they just can't recall.

Willard is one person who remembers hunkering and often mentions it to me in the worst possible places. You could be in line at the funeral home and the guy behind you will start talking about "the good ole days" even if your momma's in line with you. This is part of the male bonding experience: embarrass your friends in public.

"Remember when we took those three girls to the Soap Stone Mine when we were supposed to be studying for exams?" he'll ask you breathlessly, like he just can't contain himself even though the preacher is standing behind him.

"Uh, sir, I think you have the wrong person," you stutter, not because it's been thirty years since you've seen this stupid joker and you've forgotten his name, but because your wife is staring at you with great interest.

That's how Willard is. You get in line at a wedding reception and there he is, asking you about hunkering.

Some things are better left in the past and hunkering is one of these. People grow up and change. Some change for the better and some for the worse. But memories like getting stark naked and sitting in a cool mountain stream with a case of beer on a hundred-degree day are better forgotten. Or better still, denied.

So I just avoid Willard at most public functions, especially on hot summer days, because these seem to bring out his best memories. It's always beyond me why some people can't remember what they ate for breakfast but can remember every moss covered rock thirty years ago.

But hunkering is definitely an old Southern tradition, that's for sure.

Then there's noodling. I don't know who first came

up with noodling, but they were mighty hungry, even hungrier than the guy who first came up with coon hunting.

Willard first introduced me to noodling several years ago, but only because I thought it had something to do with pasta. You really have to be careful around people like Willard. You can think you're going out for a quiet afternoon of drag racing and end up at Daytona.

The word noodling, for you novices, is derived from two different root words: first, the Greek "nood", meaning basically "one who is liable to lose his hand up to the wrist"; and secondly, the Chinese "ling", as in "ding-a-ling".

Willard had read about noodling in *Wildlife in North Carolina* which, along with *Trailer Life*, encompasses his entire library. He had found a local man, Oscar MacGinness (also known as "Nub") to teach him how to do it.

After listening to Nub explain this noodling process, it dawned on me that noodling involves a highly deranged person wading waist deep out into a pond or river, searching under the bank with his bare hands and pulling out snapping turtles, hopefully by the tail.

I'll tell you what, you have to have a mighty powerful hankering for turtle meat to go noodling. I guess if I had just crossed the Sahara and come across this pond and there were no crawdads or tadpoles in it to eat, I might give noodling a shot. That doesn't explain why I went with Willard that day, but you have to know Willard and you have to understand the male psyche.

Willard's love for turtle meat is exceeded only by his love for frog legs. On the way to the grocery store one day, he had spotted an old snapper crossing the road, and stopped and thrown him into the trunk of his car. On the way home, he was waylaid by several yard sales and by the time he had pulled into his driveway, the turtle had ripped up the insulation, wiring, two fishing rods, a pair of boots and was fixing to gnaw through the back seat. This was a circumstance that Willard found difficult to explain to his wife, who had sent him to the grocery store for something quick and easy for supper.

Then there's the male bonding thing. You never tell your buddy you've had this deathly fear of water ever since you saw Psycho and that Jaws did nothing to alleviate it. You just grin when he says 'lets go noodling' like you could bite the head off a water moccasin.

Our first (and I might mention, our last) noodling expedition involved Willard, Hoyle and me and a local pond. While studying up on noodling, Willard had read in Wildlife in North Carolina that if something latched onto your hand you should relax and not jerk away. That way, whatever critter had hold of you would let go and not chew your hand, arm and shoulder to smithereens.

This, said Willard, seemed to be the key to the whole noodling business.

We more or less let Willard lead the way, he being the noodling expert and Hoyle and I not possessing the patience or the reserve to relax a great deal in muddy water up to our arm pits.

Willard said noodling was not about food, but about adventure. Anybody could go to the Food Lion and pick up some turtle meat, he said.

"There are just some things a man has to do," Willard remarked, "just because it's there."

I looked around and Hoyle wasn't there anymore. He had stepped into a hole and had disappeared from sight, leaving only a wake like a large motorboat.

"Tell Hoyle to quit flogging around so under water," said Willard. "He'll scare away the turtles."

This adventure went on for about half an hour, until I was getting so water logged I didn't think I could move anymore. Then Willard poked around under the bank and finally managed to noodle out an old wine bottle and what we later determined to be a mighty irritated muskrat.

"I thought you weren't supposed to jerk your hand away," Hoyle wheezed after we'd all gotten our breath.

"Don't bother me with details," gasped Willard, "just help me out of this tree."

"Let go of my leg," I said, "and I will."

I sure hope Willard doesn't get behind me at the Food Lion and ask me if I remember being up the tree with him, Hoyle, the muskrat and the wine bottle.

I'll deny everything.

The Money Log

Money management can be quite frustrating, due mainly to the fact that if there is any at all of the former, there seems to be a total lack of the latter. It always appears that if one has money, one has an uncontrollable urge to blow it. In financial circles, and especially on Wall Street, this is known as "burning a hole in your pocket". Or, as Jackie Mason said, "I have enough money to last me the rest of my life unless I buy something."

Good financial planning is often nothing more than common sense. Basically, this means spending less than you make, unless you are a government agency, then you can disregard this advice.

Most of us have received our W-2's at the end of the year, showing us how much we earned. This is always a revelation to see how much we made and how little we have left. If you have this problem, you probably need to learn the basics of cash flow management, which essentially means that what little cash you have manages to flow by faster than the Mississippi at flood stage.

Any money management plan must begin with good record keeping. This, along with good solid planning, cash flow management, protection of assets (known in the trade as covering your assets) and praying for a big win in the Virginia lottery, can bring you financial security.

Most of my record keeping is based on the pile system, a convenient method which places all documents in the order in which they are received.

A financial diary is also an asset, especially when you can't remember where you piled your pile file. I have included here excerpts from my last year's diary:

January 1: Decide to set financial goals for New Year. Vow to win Publisher's Clearing House Sweepstakes.

February 9: File income tax return. (Albert Einstein said "The hardest thing in the world to understand is income tax." I swear, he really said this.) I realize upon filing taxes that we are due $34.61 state tax refund.

February 10: Begin to plan how to spend state refund.

February 11: Spend state refund.

April 2: State announces that due to lack of funds, state tax refunds will be late this year.

April 9: Initiate plan to save large sums of money in case sweepstakes plan falls through. Sandra has mentioned that she vaguely remembers year we went to Myrtle Beach on vacation. I can't remember this far back, but agree that our goal will be a weekend at the beach this summer. Our plan is to save all our change at the end of the day and put it into a money jar.

April 10: Raid money jar for snack.

April 11: Raid money jar for gas.

June 1: Finally receive $34.61 state tax refund.

June 2: Car, having exceeded warranty by two days, falls apart, all its foreign plastic parts having gone to car heaven.

July 4: Vacation time approaches. Check money jar. Find $1.97 in pennies and several I.O.U.s. Spend $1.97 on snack.

July 5: Decide to spend vacation at local park.

July 6: Face reality that someone else has won sweepstakes. Begin Plan B. Look under couch and car seats for loose change.

December 20: Federal Reserve lowers discount rate to 3.5 percent, lowest in 27 years. This means that the interest banks charge each other is 4 percent. Mortgage rates plummet.

December 21: In order to celebrate, I charge all Christmas gifts on credit cards.

December 22: Receive notice from credit card companies that, effective immediately, interest rates will go from a modest 18 percent to a more reasonable 21 percent. They will still continue to allow me to pay $25 a year to retain this service.

December 23: Salesman informs me that if I need to purchase "nice" present for wife, such as yacht, there is now no federal luxury tax of ten percent on those costing more than $100,000. So overwhelmed with joy, I take entire contents of money jar and splurge on Mounds Bar.

License to Listen

I've often thought that someone could make a lot of money by just listening to people. I don't mean a psychiatrist or anyone who knows what they're doing. I mean just ordinary folks who don't have a clue, but who will just listen to people and nod their heads now and then in agreement.

This field of listening seems to be a goldmine to me. Anyone who works with the public knows what I mean. People come in droves to do nothing more than talk, knowing that you are a captive listener. Their spouses have run them out of the house, never having listened to them in all their years of marriage, anyway, and the nearby coffeeshop has quit refilling their coffee for the morning. So here they come to you, hungry for a listener. And they don't just talk about everyday stuff like the weather or crops. They want to tell you personal stuff like itches and odor problems.

I think there's a future in listening.

This dawned on me one day quite innocently while working in the post office. A stranger came in, bought some stamps, and started talking.

"Does your underwear ride up on you?" he asked,

then without waiting for an answer, continued. "Mine rides up on me bad. I don't know what causes it. Must run in the family. Had a great-aunt who nearly died from it one summer. Came in from horseback riding with her bra down around her waist and her panties up around her neck. Like to have choked to death before we could cut her loose.

"I don't think it's the brand, neither. I've tried several different brands and they're all the same. It's that foreign elastic they're using now. It won't stay put. Moves like it's got a life of its own."

Well, I realized right away that the American people are a lonely people. Here was this guy, leaning up against the wall of the post office, picking his teeth with a straw, telling me his deepest, darkest secrets. I bet he hadn't even discussed this problem with his wife.

"What's wrong, honey? You've turned a little blue in the face. Underwear riding up on you?"

"Uh, no dear, I must've swallowed my straw. Well, got to go down to the post office and buy a stamp."

Men seem to need this listening service more so than women. Women have their own outlets to get things off their chests. There are, however, some women who still fix their own hair who are in great need of listeners. Like the one who came in the other day.

"Husband left me today. That's all right, though, 'cause I got me a boy friend down in Carthage. Been going with him two years. My second kid is his. My husband drank like a fish...course, I do, too. Got drunk one night and woke up with a tattoo, see, it's right here. My daddy abused me real bad. Beat me with a tire tool. I finally blew his brains out. The law thought it was suicide..."

"Yes, ma'am, that's nice, but I've got to go. My underwear is riding up on me."

The trouble is, we who work with the public can't go anywhere. Basically we're trapped, even if we're really busy at the moment. People don't mind watching work, though. A lot of people can watch work all day long and be as fresh that night as they were in the morning.

So if we're going to have to listen and do our jobs, too, we who work with the public should be able to make something off this listening to people.

We could put our shingle outside our businesses: "Listening $60 an hour. Personal problems $70. Itches $80. Free coffee and weather report." I don't think we'd need a couch, cause these folks seem more relaxed just standing around like one of the regular customers not attracting too much attention, except that you see them so much you'd think they worked there, too.

This seems like such a good thing to me that the State Department of Revenue has probably thought of it, too, and probably has a license fee for it. As a matter of fact, they'd probably require you to complete a course at your local technical institute before you could be a certified listener. Then you'd have to pass a test and have to belong to a Listening Association and get a newsletter every month and go back now and then for re-certification. And you'd have specialists within the Listening field. You'd have your Itch Listeners, your Hemorrhoid Specialists, listeners trained in marital problems or exotic diseases.

Then I'd have to hire a secretary to dole out appointments and people would get so frustrated from waiting in line for someone to listen to them that they might go home and talk to their own spouses for a change.

Nah, that last part is a little too far out.

And They Call It A "Festival"

It only comes once a year.

This is a big consolation every day of the year but one. On this particular year when Jamie was in grade school I had promised to be better prepared when the fateful day arrived. I was going to exercise, find some program to work on lower body strength, for this was a day when upper body strength meant nothing.

The secret, I had learned the hard way, was in the toes, feet, shins and knees. Weak spots, for sure, but I was certain they could be protected. I had also planned to stand for hours in a hot, stuffy closet to get acclimated. To go to the bank around the first of the month and practice waiting in line. To offer to be a sheet salesman at white sales. To jog. To take mega-vitamins.

But the aforesaid day arrived and I had done none of these. It was Friday the 13th, appropriately, and the Fall Festival was again upon us.

The anticipation on Jamie's face was tremendous. Sandra and I were a bit more reserved. Funereal at best.

We arrived at the school. The nearest parking space appeared to be just south of Somalia. We finally found a closer space, within a bean-bag toss of the gym.

"Oh, Momma," Jamie exclaimed as the car rolled to a halt. "Mrs. Kuhn wanted me to ask you if you wanted to work in a booth..."

It wasn't that Jamie had forgotten, it was just that she was being thoughtful. She had waited until we arrived to announce this so that Sandra wouldn't be stuck working in a dull booth all night and could share in all the fun on the gym floor.

Custer probably had scouts like this looking after him, too.

The cafeteria was almost empty when we entered. Jamie had opted for a hot dog in the gym. All the way, no drink. Perhaps she knows something about the cafeteria food that we don't, I thought.

But the chicken pie was delicious, as usual. The salad was gone by the time we arrived, but I had seen Hoyle's wife's tray piled up like the Pyramids, so I figured there would be some shortages. Two rolls were substituted for the salad, a fair trade, because they were delectable. When I was in school, all we had was fish sticks. Times have changed.

A tall female figure appeared behind me. I braced myself for some teacher to admonish me to finish my Lima beans. I moved them around some with my fork to make it look like I'd been eating them. She only smiled and poured more tea.

Jamie was squirming, watching the clock closely. She might have felt that we were stalling the inevitable.

"We only have 30 more minutes," she informed me.

"That much, huh?" I replied. The clock read 7:30. I remembered time dragging like this at my school, too. "Don't worry," I assured her. "We've got a hour and a half." She brightened considerably.

The gym was packed, hot and stuffy in spots and cold and drafty in others. It was slightly reassuring to know that some things didn't change.

Jamie had eight tickets. We made a quick tour of the gym. Richard Petty could not have maneuvered though the crowd better than Jamie. I was reminded of the winter days I had once attempted to follow beagles through briar patches and brush piles. This was Jamie's world. She could look almost everyone in the eye and talk to them, face to face.

I was engulfed in a sea of heads, surging around me three to four feet deep, an undercurrent of arms and legs, a rip tide of little shoes.

A herd of something trooped across my feet. I made a mental note to wear steel-toed boots next year. I turned to see where Jamie had gone and caught cotton candy in the face.

After three whirlwind tours around the gym, Jamie settled on a booth. It was the old shell game played with miniature pumpkins. Jamie had a winner on the second try. She beamed up at me as if to say "This is a cinch," but her words were drowned by hundreds of little voices.

She handed me a red ticket.

"What's this for?" I yelled over the crowd.

"You turn these in for prizes," she replied, patiently overlooking my ignorance. "Like Coke bottles stretched real long, or false teeth."

I tucked it safely in a shirt pocket and every now and then checked nervously to make sure it was still there.

We passed the Moon Walk. Last year Jamie had begged to try it. This year it was ignored. Perhaps a year had matured her, and besides, there were no prizes to win there. Only sweaty, puffy kids bouncing around.

The booth she most wanted to try had been closed. Someone had made off with the bean bags. She tried the paper airplane toss and put one in the hanger the first time. Another red ticket tucked safely away.

"You do have two of them," she reminded me. I assured her I did.

One of my shoes became attached to the floor. Someone had lost their gum and I had found it. I bumped into Hoyle. He had found one of his kids, then lost her looking for the other.

"I'm just tagging along with Jamie," I explained, pointing down to the child whose hand I was clutching. He wasn't Jamie. He wasn't even a little girl. I released his hand and he looked quite relieved. Jamie was motioning me to wait in line with her at another bean bag game. We were either sixth in line or sixteenth, it was hard to tell. This wasn't your everyday line.

There is no way to explain a fall festival line to the uninitiated. After about fifteen minutes we were still closer to the Pantry than we were to the bean bag game. But the line was moving. It was getting longer. And I noticed an entirely different set of kids in front of us than before, and some had formed auxiliary lines off to the sides.

After about a half an hour in line, there was finally one little girl between us and the booth. She immediately threw all three bean bags over the target and behind the folding bleachers. Teachers scraped and searched for them furiously. They retrieved them just before mayhem broke out in the line.

No red ticket here. We moved on to the golf booth. After another appropriate wait, Jamie's turn came. She grabbed the golf club in a rather unorthodox grip, much like holding a knife and fork, and swung away. A complete miss. Behind us, a man laughed. I wondered if he would like his face stuck through the bean bag target.

Jamie drilled the next ball right into the hole. She accepted her red ticket and grinned triumphantly at me. I speculated that Arnold Palmer might want to know about that grip.

We found Sandra, seated on a table in the midst of spilled Coke, crushed cups and ice. I'll never be that tired, I thought, to sit in that mess. Someone mentioned that other schools in the county have a Spring Fling to complement their Fall Festival. I sat down.

The crowd was thinning now, freeing up some walking room. Jamie had three tickets out of eight tries. She seemed satisfied.

She picked up her prizes in the music room. They were displayed in tubs, a veritable treasure trove of plastic and cellophane. Jamie selected two rubber spiders, two yo-yo's and a tic-tac-toe game.

She skipped to the car.

"Did you have fun?" I asked.

"Oh, yes," she giggled, dangling a black spider in the air menacingly.

Then it was worth it, I thought.

Litters of Critters

It seems that every fall when there begins to be a chill in the air and the leaves start to turn, the critters start to want to come into our house.

I didn't mind a few critters now and then when I was single. That was the price you paid for leaving the door open all night. But now that I'm married, I have obligations. Like Sandra.

There's not too much Sandra is afraid of. For instance, I would feel sorry for a battalion of Hell's Angels with muddy boots trying to track across her kitchen floor. And she once actually chased a would-be car thief. The guy would've stolen her car had it been tuned up, but instead Sandra heard him grinding away on the starter and chased him across the town hall parking lot into Lowe's Foods where the police later arrested him. I hear he was glad to be in the more beneficent arms of the law.

But there are many things that frighten Sandra and most of them either crawl around on four little feet or slither on their bellies. And with autumn the time of year that snakes and things like to follow you home like puppies, Sandra gets a little antsie.

It's a good idea not to mention to your friends that

you are afraid of critters. They all immediately feel obligated to tell you the most horrible rat or snake story they know.

"Aunt Millie...you remember 'Blind Aunt Millie'? Went to bed one night and the rats ate her eyeballs clean out of the sockets and Uncle George never heard a thang."

"Oh, rats chewed Grandma's kneecaps plum off while she napped on the sofa."

"A snake jumped Momma's sister on the way to the clothesline and swallowed her whole. All they found was the clothes basket and her false teeth."

"I knew a lady what was sitting on the edge of her bed one night and rattlesnakes crawled right up her underwear. Had been living in the mattress for years."

"That's nothing. I know a woman who was sitting on the commode and a python came right up through the sewer and scared her so bad that she won't go nowhere, especially to the bathroom, without her hoe..."

And these are the tame stories. I don't know what it is about people, but if you'll admit a fear, they'll make it worse.

Sandra had made the mistake of walking into the bathroom one night just as a mouse also made his entrance. I had trapped the offending creature against my better judgment, because I was aware that you can get into deep trouble over actions like this. There are actually animal rats, er, rights activists who would take you to court over such a matter. I had read that the Humane Society in New Jersey had charged a guy named Frank Balun with cruelty to animals for whacking a rat with a broom handle and I wasn't too happy over this prospect.

After secretly hauling off the carcass, I had boarded up every crack, crevice, nook and cranny so tight that we almost asphyxiated. I had just calmed Sandra's fears to the point where she could go into the bathroom again without an axe, when in walked the plumber one day.

"I don't like to work on your plumbing," he remarked innocently. "There are too many snakes under your house."

After reviving Sandra, I guess he must have felt it best to at least offer some solutions to the problem, so he mentioned that mothballs will keep any self-respecting snake away from your house. Besides, he added sheepishly, he had only seen a couple of snake skins under the house.

Well, you might as well have told Patton you had only seen a couple of German Panzer units nearby. The next morning, as I was drinking coffee, I heard a "plop, plop, plop" sound coming from under the house. It sounded as if someone were throwing gravel-sized somethings to every corner of the crawl space. Being well-versed in these situations, I did not go down to the basement. I waited for Sandra to come upstairs.

"I've got a box and a half of them under this part of the house," she said. " I need you to help me scatter the rest under the other part. It's lower."

It was fortunate that the stores in town didn't have but three pounds of mothballs in stock. We went to the basement. It looked like it had snowed.

"I figured if a few mothballs would keep snakes away, three boxes full would keep everything away," she said gleefully.

We went back upstairs. The air conditioner came on. The house began to smell like great-aunt Helga's winter clothes. Outside you could see moths leaving the basement in droves. There was nowhere for the smell to go because the house was hermetically sealed, so we had to open windows to get some fresh air.

"If you leave those windows open," Sandra said, "won't snakes be able to crawl through the screen?"

After awhile it was decided that we either move out or I would try to recover all the mothballs in the crawl space before we suffocated. I donned some old clothes and started to crawl under the house when I heard a scream coming from inside the house.

"Leaping Lizards!" Sandra was hollering. I ran into the house.

"This thing's as big as an iguana." By the sound of her voice, it seemed that she was hanging from the light fixture on the ceiling of the bedroom.

Several things immediately ran through my mind. Burglars would not have caused Sandra to scream. It must be another critter.

I don't like to just run in head-on into these situations without being armed. I didn't know what creatures the mothballs might have stirred up. Snakes entered my mind. A neighbor called me years ago screaming that a snake was in her house.

I grabbed a hoe, which is the recommended weapon of choice by the Snake Killers Association of America and ran next door expecting a cobra to jump me any minute. There, coiled up under her sink, was a giant (and for all I knew, deadly poisonous) black snake.

I was just trying to figure out how to get the hoe under the sink when she grabbed the handle.

"Can't you just put it in a pillow case and carry it outside?" she begged.

"Do I look like Marlin Perkins?" I asked.

Luckily, the snake slithered back down the drain

pipe hole while we were having this enlightening conversation.

And you have to be careful about which weapon you choose in fighting these critters. My brother, panicking after spotting a snake in the hallway, grabbed an axe and chopped up his floor pretty good. I don't know what happened to the snake. He probably died laughing.

You want to have enough weapon to do the job without going overboard. Julie will spray the entire contents of an economy sized can of Raid on one poor spider. The poor thing looks like he's trying to get out of a snow bank.

Frank Balun evidently believes in the effectiveness of a broom handle in situations like this, so I grabbed a broom.

"Hurry up," Sandra was yelling. "This thing looks like it came from Jurassic Park."

I arrived in the bedroom to find an ashen-faced wife braced against the dresser like a bull moose might be trying to escape from beneath it.

"What is it?" I asked, almost afraid to know.

"It's one of *those* lizards," she answered, putting a little extra emphasis on "those" to let me know she had warned me of the lizard problem before. It seems that "those" lizards had been congregating in the sun outside the house for weeks. It was only a matter of time before one would want to come inside to use our restroom facilities.

"We can't kill it," I told her. I hated to break the news to her, especially at a time like this, but it had to come out.

"What do you mean 'we can't kill it'?" she screamed, a slight hint of smoke coming out her ears.

"Frank Balun," I said. "The guy who was arrested for killing a rat. I'm not going to jail over a lizard."

"Nobody will ever know," she said solemnly. "It will never leave this room. Now, let that monster have it before he gets away."

"They might give Frank Balun a year in prison and $2500 in fines for whacking that rat over the head," I repeated.

"You've got the money," Sandra pleaded, "and you've got plenty of time. Go ahead and bash him. Besides, if he doesn't go, I do."

Seeing a different light on the subject, I removed the offending lizard from the premises. Because of pending criminal cases in New Jersey involving rat killers, the rest of the story cannot be repeated here.

But after the lizard was gone, Sandra educated me on how this is the time of year varmints start wanting to come inside your home and spend the winter with you.

"If there's one," she said, "you *know* there's more of them."

I just hope the stores don't run out of mothballs before winter gets here.

The Wreck of Old Number 31

In dentist lingo, it was Tooth Number 31 that was causing me all the pain. I had been minding my own business chewing away at a wad of gum when the sharp, stabbing pain shot through my jaw in waves like the Marines landing on Iwo Jima.

Dentists number your teeth instead of naming them so that you don't become so attached to them. It's easier to say "We're going to drill Tooth Number 31" than to say "It's old George. He'll have to go."

Tooth Number 31 is a molar of the lower jaw with roots like an oak tree. These roots are hooked directly to the brain and the spinal column and have direct dial to every nerve in your body. These nerves are particularly allergic to hot and cold or even slight breezes. This is why it's a good idea to keep the enamel around them as long as possible.

When the pain struck me, I was sure it was more than one tooth. It seemed like every tooth west of the Pecos was in agony including my ear and part of my chin. I figured it was at least Teeth 16 through 31. This was before I knew that molar roots go clean to Honduras.

There is a universal tooth law that toothaches should

occur only on weekends. There should be a dentist emergency room for people in life threatening pain. But, in my case, I should have expected it. I had criminally neglected my teeth for several years and it was only right that they should rebel. They could have rebelled on a Monday, though.

I resigned myself that I would have to wait until a weekday to call a dentist. Then, as the pain intensified, I decided that I would show up on the dentist's door early that Monday morning as soon as they unlatched the doors. I would not be too proud to beg. I would plead with the receptionist as I wrapped my arms around her understanding ankles. I would even cry, which was getting easier and easier to do with each passing hour.

Basically, receptionists are people who take cold showers. The military takes receptionists and automatically puts them in the Special Forces, no additional training required. Dentists hire these people because of their ability to look in the face of raw, exposed nerves and not wince, but to smile sweetly and say "Yes, we have an appointment in May...of next year."

All weekend long, the pain got continually worse. I was popping pain pills like raisins and they were doing about as much good. Sunday night I promised never again to break another dentist appointment. I promised to quit smoking. Never mind that I had quit smoking years ago.

At 9:00 Monday morning, the receptionist opened the dentist's office door and I fell in at her feet. She took me right back to the dentist.

He looked into my mouth, asked "is this the one?" and gently tapped Tooth Number 31. As the nurse peeled me from the ceiling, he explained that the tooth was abscessed and that I would have to have a root canal done by an endodontist. The endodontist couldn't see me until Friday.

So all week long I popped pain pills and penicillin and looked forward to my root canal. I had so much pain killer in me I could have had an appendectomy and never felt a thing. Yet the tooth still hurt.

Many people told me about their root canals. Terrible things, they said. Some people had even lived through them.

I didn't care. I didn't care that some people had almost passed out from pain *while* having a root canal. I didn't care that the root canal was a form of torture devised by the Sioux Indians. I was looking forward to my root canal.

Finally Friday morning came. I bounced into the endodontist's office with a smile on my face and a song in my heart. I told the receptionist how happy I was to be there. I shook the patients' hands. I hugged the endodontist.

The root canal went fine. They use little rotorooters to burrow out the pulp from your roots then pack the holes with cement.

The endodontist then gave me more penicillin and some high powered pain pills "if I needed them." I assured him that nothing could be worse than the pain I had already suffered. And I went home to plan the rest of my day.

I didn't figure on Hiroshima. About 12:30 it hit. The Royal Canadian Mounted Police on track shoes. Fourteen sore thumbs. Someone pulling your fingernails out one by one.

I grabbed the pain killers. The bottle said to take

one or two every four to six hours. I took four to six every one or two hours.

Never have I looked so forward to something to be let down so badly. No wonder the Geneva Convention banned root canal as a form of warfare and replaced it with poisonous gas.

All of this because of dental neglect on old Number 31.

If you have a choice between losing a tooth and a root canal, go with the root canal. But if you have a choice between a root canal and execution by firing squad, you may want to take some time to think about it.

Inventions

Someone once said that necessity is the mother of invention. Someone else said that getting caught is the mother of invention. Whatever the case, the average inventor is rarely appreciated.

When the initial caveman brought home that first fire into his cave, what did his wife say?

"Don't bring that thing in here, I just vacuumed."

This first fire was probably looked upon with suspicion, just as are many discoveries and inventions. The wife surely didn't like it because it shed light on 12,000 cockroaches lurking around the bed and under the chest of drawers (the forerunner of the chester drawers in the South). The man didn't like it because it made the cave too hot. It also brought a new, never before tried, concept in food preparation, one that has been handed down carefully from one generation to another: burned biscuits.

The cavekids didn't much like this discovery because now they had to haul wood into the cave and clean out the ashes. But it provided much needed light with which to read the T.V.*Guide* so the concept of fire caught on and has persisted down through the ages.

Century after century fire has proved handy in heating homes, torching witches and burning down Chicago.

All this makes me wonder what grandpa caveman thought of all this. He probably talked to the little cavekids about how all he had to keep warm with was wooly mammoth hides and homemade quilts while he walked to school all the way across Siberia.

And if the poor guy who first brought home the fire was met with skepticism, imagine what happened to the first wheel. It probably ended up in the first junk yard.

Here's this caveman who has been sent out to bring back a rump roast and some potatoes for supper and he walks into the house with a wheel. His wife is still trying to get the hang of the fire he brought home the week before and the babies are hollering for their MTV and here hubbie stands with a wheel. This probably resulted in the invention of the doghouse.

Of course, the cavekids liked the idea of the wheel immediately and asked for the keys right away. This resulted in the invention of ulcers.

Soon, someone else came along with another wheel and created the first skateboard. Then followed the first broken leg.

The invention of the wheel can't be taken lightly, though. Without the wheel, how could you ground your kid? Take away his horse? We also wouldn't have potholes, garage sales or gasoline tax. We owe a lot to the inventor of the wheel. Because of him, or her, we can sit in traffic for 45 minutes to go to work to earn the money to pay the car payment, car insurance and car wash.

When it comes to inventions, Ben Franklin with his stupid kite ranks right up there with the wheel guy. Not to be satisfied with a good fire on a cold night, Ben has got to go and discover electricity. Why would an otherwise intelligent man go out in the rain with a kite just to discover something so expensive?

At least the discovery of electricity gave the meter readers something to do. It also came in handy when Thomas Edison invented the light bulb, which in turn made black outs possible, a condition occurring most frequently to people after reading their electric bills.

I could probably forgive Henry Ford for the wheel and Franklin for the kilowatt hour, but Alexander Graham Bell is a different story.

Alex Bell is a man who evidently loved misery. He had no phone bill in his early childhood. He could take a shower pretty much without interruption, unless the telegraph went off. On his days off, he could hang around the house without salesmen calling him every five minutes. He was never put on hold. It's doubtful he ever got a wrong number. He didn't have to endure numerous and sundry AT&T, Sprint and MCI commercials over and over and over again.

Bell must have had a great desire for an obscene call, though, because he went out and invented the telephone. Before the telephone came along, no one had the uncontrollable desire to dial your number at midnight and breathe into the receiver. Alexander Graham Bell created a whole new breed of perverts: vinyl siding salesmen.

Henry Ford invented the automobile so that he could get away from the telephone and what did Alex Bell do? He invented the car phone. When the vinyl siding salesmen get your car phone number, where will you hide?

I miss the Fuller Brush salesman much like grandpa caveman missed his wooly mammoth hide. We need a moratorium on inventions, a freeze, a time to catch our breath. Give me time to figure out the answering machine before you throw the VCR at me. Let me at least master the eight-track tape player before you go inventing anything else just yet.

Moving, Moving, Moving

We have moved enough in our lifetimes to qualify for membership in the International Gypsy's Union.

People will tell you that building a new house will break up a marriage quicker than squeezing the toothpaste in the middle. But believe me, it's the moving that does it, not the building.

We are a nation on the move. It boggles the mind to think that a hundred years ago, great grandpa loaded all the family belongings into a covered wagon and took off for Kansas. He not only took grandma, who was pregnant, but also the eleven kids, the green vase General Washington gave his father and probably the aquarium, too. The twelfth child was born in Kentucky and by the time they reached Topeka, another was on the way. And nothing was broken.

It must have taken 400 people to move us across town. At least that's how many we had to feed. I suspect some came in off the streets just to get a meal.

If you have an over-abundance of friends and want some of them to disappear, you can either loan them a book or move. Friends get mighty scarce at moving time. The conversation goes something like this:

"Well, we're about ready to move again. Probably in a couple of weeks."

Friend's left eye begins to twitch uncontrollably.

"Do you still have that 20-foot couch?" he asks.

"You mean the one we had to hoist up through the second floor window, then lower down the stairway and turn at a 90-degree angle to get into the living room?" I answer. "The very one that mashed someone's kneecap between the banister and the couch, and we thought we'd have to have it surgically removed? The one that Sandra then decided should go in the den, not the living room?"

"That's the one," he says, mysteriously rubbing his kneecap. "You know, the wife and I have been planning a trip for that week. When did you say you were moving?"

"Sometime in April, probably."

"Yeah, we were going to be gone all of April. More than likely all spring. And summer, too."

Since I have had so many moving experiences over the years, I feel qualified to share some tips with those of you who may be moving soon, or who are just looking for a quick way to end your marriage. Here are some tips:

You have about three choices when moving. You can call on your friends to help, that is if you have an over abundance of them and don't mind losing a few and watching grown men cry doesn't effect you.

You can hire a mover but, unlike friends, they charge. They won't eat as much, however, or make snide remarks about your nouveau poor furnishings or the lint under the refrigerator.

Or, you can do it alone and break all that stuff by yourself.

It is wise to tape all mirrors. This way all the glass won't fall out and cut you when it shatters. There's no need to wrap cheap stuff like the vase Aunt Joy bought at Rose's and gave you last Christmas. Anvils break before this stuff does. And there's really no need to wrap valuable glassware like the vase General Washington gave the family back in 1780 because it's gonna break no matter what. You can, however, mark boxes containing glass "Fragile" so that your helpers know which ones to play catch with.

One of the bigger lies around is the statement that "One good thing about moving is that you get rid of a lot of junk". I can safely debunk this theory by walking out to our storage shed and showing you the hula hoop, a flat Wolfpack basketball (not unlike the team), about 93 old Christmas tree stands, a plastic snow sled (in case we have plastic snow this winter), a weed eater that quit eating weeds three moves ago, stuffed toy beaver and bag full of assorted friends (some with eyes) and a patented Carocelle Dishwasher, a contraption that you hook up to the water spigot to wash your dishes.

When you move, you might as well console yourself to the fact that you're not going to throw anything away. If you were, you would have done it years ago. So don't even dare to sift through the kitchen cabinet drawer that contains all the mementoes of the years in your old house. Just take the entire drawer of coke caps, empty match pads, screws, nails, partial decks of cards, wire, string and receipts and dump the contents into a corresponding drawer in your new home.

No matter how rough the going gets, you can always count on a couple of old friends to help. Maybe they're secretly looking for stuff they loaned you years ago or maybe they're gluttons for punishment.

I can always count on Walter and Ed to help. Walter and I tend to study the situation and stand and wonder if a bicycle will fit on the truck between the chairs and the night stand. Ed just picks up the bicycle, chest of drawers and two stools, and fits them right in.

A typical conversation between Walt and I might go something like this:

"If I can just get this solid oak dresser with all its contents still in it and its marble top over that small hump in the doorway..."

"EEEEE...that small hump was my toe."

"Whoops, sorry about mashing you against the window sill with that couch."

"That's OK, we had given up having any more children, anyway."

"Where's all the garbage bags full of clothes we put on the truck?"

"Oh, I threw them off at the dump."

If you happen to be moving any time soon, you can take heart in the fact that millions of Americans have safely moved before you and, although they will everyone disappear on the day you need them, you can always call United Van Lines.

Halloween

The ancient festival of Halloween had its roots in Europe during the dark ages when simple peasant folk, trying to take their minds off the horrors of the upcoming elections, dressed like witches, vampires and zombies. Later, when it became legal for politicians to suck the blood out of the local populace, vampire costumes became less popular.

Some strange acting people in costumes will come knocking at your door begging for handouts around the end of October, but pay no attention to them. They are politicians. The real trick-or-treaters will be kids, although some politicians act like children, so be careful.

Halloween tends to get some bad press because of its pagan origins. The early Celtics began their new year on November first and celebrated the last night of October as "old-year's night" or the night of all witches. The Romans had a harvest festival about this same time in honor of Pomona, their goddess of fruit. The Celtics went on to much fame, although they have slipped over the last few years without Larry Bird.

But none of us celebrate Halloween as a pagan festival. What matters is what is in the heart and Halloween centers on what is in the heart of most Americans: getting.

There's always someone out to stop Halloween. I remember one year the "Iowa City School District Equity-Affirmative Action Advisory Committee" suggested that parents should be mindful of their children's costumes "to avoid unpleasant and hurtful situations."

I remember these hurtful situations well from my Halloween days as a child. We had two basic costumes when I was growing up:

1. The ghost costume, made from an old sheet.

2. The paper bag costume, made from a paper bag.

Both were created by cutting three to four holes in a sheet or a bag and putting them over your head.

These costumes looked good on the drawing board and weren't too bad when you first put them on in the house before going out to loot, er, trick-or-treat. B u t once you stepped out into the darkness, you were as blind as a bat. The holes in the sheet or bag never lined up quite properly with your eyes after you left the house. This resulted in your being able to locate clothes lines with the efficiency of radar. I've hit so many clothes lines running through peoples' backyards that I still have permanent scars on my neck.

Nowadays, kids would be afraid of running through backyards because of some silly fear of getting shot, but we did it with regularity on Halloween.

The sheet costume had one other drawback, too. It was always longer than you were and tended to trip you up, especially right after you'd turned someone's garbage can over.

Kids today don't say "Trick-or-treat" too much. Many of them just stand at your door with their plastic pumpkins held out in front of them. When we went trick-or-treating, we carried giant paper grocery bags. If we filled up one bag, we could always take the one off our head for a spare.

If we didn't get any goodies at a house, or the unfortunate inhabitants hadn't left their porch light on, we usually turned over their porch furniture. We never threw any eggs or toilet paper, mainly because we couldn't afford either.

The little kids now say "Happy Halloween", which is a cute thing to say. It also leads me to believe that they aren't the type kids who would turn over your porch furniture.

We always hated getting fruit, popcorn or pennies at Halloween. We were mainly after chocolate because we could get fruit anytime of year. As a matter of fact, we subsisted on fruit for most of the year and normally weren't allowed near any chocolate unless it was a dire emergency. That's why we liked Halloween so much. It was the only night of the year we were allowed to eat an entire five pound grocery bag full of Milk Duds at one sitting.

I have a feeling a lot of these dads escorting their kids around on Halloween are in it for the Milk Duds. Last year I heard a little boy ask his dad: "How many more houses do we have to go?" I imagine his dad was thinking "just a few more boxes of Milk Duds and we'll go home."

Today, you have groups like the Iowa Advisory Committee asking children to avoid costumes that could present negative images during treat-or-treating such as gypsy, American Indian princess, elderly person, African, witch, slave, hobo and the devil. It didn't mention sheets or paper bags, so I guess these are still safe.

Sometimes the old ways are the best.

I can understand how some of these costumes might offend people. Take the gypsy lobby for instance. I would hate for a band of gypsies to descend on Congress protesting children blatantly portraying themselves as gypsies during Halloween. While in Washington, the gypsies could read some fortunes of the senators and perhaps pave their driveways.

The hobo interest is also a touchy subject. I would hate to hurt a hobo's feelings. They might hop a freight and leave town before you could explain that you meant no harm.

And there is actually a religion of witches called Wicca, that is recognized by the government and is practiced by about 200,000 witches across the United States. I would certainly hate to have 200,000 witches after me, but it could be good for the broom business.

You couldn't dress up like the devil, because you'd no doubt offend the devil worshipper crowd. I bet there's a dinosaur lobby and one for Teenage Mutant Ninga Turtles, too.

About the only thing that leaves, besides the sheets and paper bags, is to dress up like a politician and that, my friends, is a scary thought, indeed.

Scout Troop 911

The Boy Scouts of America was a major influence on my life and the lives of my friends as we were growing up. I imagine our Scout leaders, if you could locate the mental facilities in which they are now lodged, would tell you much the same thing.

The Scouts give you many skills that prepare you for later life. For instance, you learn how to deal with being wet and miserable for weekends at a time. You learn how to eat partially cooked food, warmed over a blazing fire. You are secure in the knowledge that, if locked out of the house, you can survive intact at least until supper time.

The Scouts teach you all sorts of neat knots, including the difference between a square knot and a grannie knot, in case you ever need to tie the old gal up. The Scouts are also big in crafts, teaching me how to make a billfold out of leather, one that Mom still uses as a potholder.

Many of our national leaders were Boy Scouts, although I think President Clinton was overseas during his scouting years and former vice-president Quayle was a member of the scouting reserves, ready to be called into the woods at a moment's notice.

Scouting came naturally to most of us rural kids. We weren't too proficient in many of the finer points of Scouting such as knot tying or crafts, but we were good in the woods. I could find poison ivy if any grew within miles of our campsite, for example. Willard could live on dirt for three days and actually gain weight.

Since there were no merit badges for dirt eating, Willard and many of us languished at the rank of Tenderfoot for much of our Scouting careers. Tenderfoot is similar to Buck Private, except lower.

If I remember correctly, our Patrol's name was Antelope, a name carefully chosen after rejecting Head Lice, Ardvaark and two names suggested by Assistant Scoutmaster Patterson which he thought readily described us: Toad and Rat.

We elected a kid named Thurman as our Patrol Leader mainly because his mom sent good food on camping trips. Thurman weighed in at 200 pounds and was also handy in the tug-of-war contests.

The most fun about being in the Scouts was getting to go on camporees with several other troops of Scouts. Camporee, by the way, is an Indian word roughly translated as "to sleep on damp ground with many sweaty kids."

Our patrol always split the food, with each member bringing different items. For some reason, Willard always brought the pork and beans and the candy bars. I figured it was because Willard's family couldn't afford anything else. Willard was always bumming cigarettes off the other Scouts, so I knew he was poor.

"It's strange," Willard's mom said as we loaded the food in the stationwagon for my first camporee. "Willard never eats pork and beans at home, but he always insists on having them on these camping trips."

The first night on the camporee, after we had pitched the tents, dug the latrines, built camp fires, washed dirty dishes and done other fun Scout things, Willard wanted to visit some of the other troops, especially the despised bunch from Biscoe.

"You bring the candy bars," he said as he stuffed his pockets full of cans of pork and beans.

I had no idea why we were going to visit the hated Biscoeans, but knowing that Scouts are friendly, I went along.

We chatted with the Biscoe troop for awhile and per Willard's instructions, I shared the candy bars with them. Just as soon as we had gotten comfortable, Willard was ready to go. When I was slow about getting to my feet, Willard jerked me into the shadows.

Running through the dark woods, we both tripped on a mass of wires and cables running from a generator near the stationwagon to the Scoutmaster's tent. Willard mentioned later that "roughing it" to them meant black and white TV.

We were almost back to our tent when explosions ripped the air. Wide-eyed pork and bean covered Scouts were rushing wildly in all directions.

"It's an old Indian trick," Willard explained. "You put the cans of pork and beans in the fire and eventually they explode." Willard said that while a pork and bean explosion was a frightening experience, it was rare for anyone to be killed in one. They should have had a merit badge for it, Willard was so good at it.

"Won't they suspect we did it?" I asked naively.

"No," Willard said, "they'll never know where it came from."

We awoke the next morning in the rain under a tent that had been flat on top of us most of the night, the ropes having been cut soon after we went to bed. Our supplies were scattered all over the campsite amid broken eggs and several cans of beans poured over our clothes.

"I'm certainly glad they didn't know it was us," I said as we untangled ourselves.

The whole adventure added to lessons learned that would later benefit me in life. Beware of geeks bearing gifts. And never sit too close to the fire.

To Sleep, Perhaps To Dream

If there's anything I'm an expert at, it's sleeping. I can go to sleep anywhere, anytime. I've slept on brick sidewalks in the Army, I've slept on the ground in the rain. I've slept in jungle hammocks, in the car, on buses, in airplanes. Occasionally, I've slept in beds.

I could probably sleep through a nuclear attack. Every now and then, Sandra will wake me by lightly tapping on my head with some metallic object to ask me if I think we should evacuate the house just because hurricane force winds have uprooted trees in the yard. If she would just not bother me, I'd never know that the Piedmont was flooded knee deep by torrential rains with much loss of life.

But of all places I have slept, no sleep beats the sleep you get in your trusty recliner, preferably in front of the TV set. You can sleep on a recliner without the TV, but it is a fitful sleep. The deepest sleep is in front of the TV with a Braves game on, or perhaps an old cowboy movie.

There seems to be a movement afoot to do away with the recliner. I first noticed this when we last moved. Then I spotted a very small newspaper article entitled

"The recline and fall of modern man". It said the single most embarrassing secret longing of American men is to own a recliner.

"The recliner is our national shame," it went on to say. "It's the clip-on tie of interior decorating...you can find recliners hidden away in spare bedrooms or in the den, in which guilty pleasures are carried out; three consecutive NBA games, viewed nearly supine, with cheap beer and assorted greasy treats at the right hand."

Well, I happen to like clip-on ties. This was the first time I was made aware that the recliner is our national shame. Here I have been living in shame all these years and just now found out about it. Looks like someone would've told me.

Sandra may have been trying to tell me something. The last time we moved, she suggested that we make one room into a sort of den/office. It's a darkly paneled room, just right for serious sleeping, with a nice view overlooking the yard. I immediately liked this idea because I'd never had a room of my very own to stack papers in and generally junk up as I wanted.

She also suggested that we move the recliner into this room. This, too, suited me fine because a darkly paneled room on a dreary rainy day that the Braves are playing is perfect for a recliner. What I didn't realize at the time, and what the article helped me understand better, is that there was no TV in the den.

Now, how is a grown man going to sleep with no TV? Of course, we have a variety of other chairs in the house adjacent to TV's. We have a glider, the modern-day version of the rocker. I have tried sleeping in this and it is not even comfortable with a double header Braves game on one TV and an old movie on the other.

We have couches, but you really don't want to stretch out on the couch while watching TV. This just admits you're planning to fall asleep all along and will only be met with "Why don't you just go on and go to bed?"

Probably the most uncomfortable chairs in any home are the dining room chairs. They are made to eat in quickly and hop out of and into a waiting recliner if possible. I don't know of anyone who has ever gone to sleep in a dining room chair and lived to tell about it.

This leaves only the bed to sleep in and this is a poor choice indeed. I had just gotten our mattress the way I wanted it. The last truly great mattress I remember was the feather bed at my great-aunt Kate's. When you sat on the edge of it, the entire thing swallowed you up like quicksand. It was like sleeping in a ditch lined with feathers. You could see the ceiling, but look right or left and all you could see was mattress.

I had almost gotten our mattress to this state of perfection. When I rolled over at night, Sandra went with me. It was like sleeping down hill and you could actually use the sides of the mattress for a pillow if you wanted. The old mattress was like putty. It fit any shape with no problem. It was certainly the next best thing to the recliner.

How Sandra could complain about such a mattress, I have no idea. It had taken years of sleeping to get it broken in just right, and now she wanted to change it. To me, it was like parting with that old recliner just because it had gotten too soft, or giving up that old baseball glove because it wasn't stiff anymore.

But Sandra's back had been giving her problems and she seemed to blame the mattress, as if that had something to do with it. My back has always given me problems. When I went to be examined to see if I was fit to be drafted into the Army, I mentioned this to one of the nice Druids and he replied that "it was nothing the Army couldn't cure."

Sure enough, I never had a minute's worth of trouble the whole time I was incarcerated in the Army. Civilian life, however, has been killing me.

I stated my case very eloquently to Sandra, noting the above details. Thus, we lived with the old mattress a year or two longer than she would have liked. However, all this happiness came to an abrupt halt not long ago.

That was the day we went down to the local Petrified Hardboard Mattress and Concrete Slab Company to pick out the new mattress. The saleslady said at first that they had nothing harder than a marble headstone, but after searching around found a mattress sized chunk of material that I figured was initially used to crush diamonds. Sandra laid down on it and pronounced it perfect.

We got it home and put it on the bed. I sat down on it and—get this—it did not move! That night I laid awake wondering how mountain climbers are able to sleep on sheer cliffs of granite.

Finally seeing that I couldn't sleep, Sandra recommended that I play a relaxation tape. She put on "The Sounds of Nature: Horrifying Electrical Storms."

"What's wrong now?" she asked.

"I can't go to sleep for fear that I'll be electrocuted," I answered. So, she replaced it with "Sounds of the Tropical Rain Forest". All night I laid there thinking tarantulas were crawling on me. Only when I realized that even a tarantula could not crawl up the sheer face of something as hard as that mattress was I able to get some sleep.

I figure in a good twenty years, if I jump up and down on it every once in awhile, I'll have this mattress broken in just right. Just my luck, though, Sandra will probably expect another new one by then.

No matter what anyone will tell you, the recliner is still king in my book and I am going right out to find me a TV set to try and cure this insomnia I've had lately.

Let It Snow

Someone needs to do a study of the way we Southerners act during the snow. It would make a better movie than anything Chevy Chase or Steve Martin ever did. You could call it "Ernest in the Snow" and make a small fortune. Any of us could play lead role.

If you have not been in the South for long, you will have to understand some of the history of Southern snows to understand how we natives act. From the Ice Age on up to the early 1900's, it was common for snow to fall, say, every fifteen minutes. People, mainly our parents and grandparents, walked to school every day in this snow for what seems like a hundred years. Ponds and rivers froze solid and freight trains drove right across them without incident.

Since the Ice Age ended, snows in the South have declined to the point that there are actually people today who have never had to walk to school in the snow. Snow is so scarce that three flakes in a row nowadays constitutes a flurry and is mandatory grounds for dismissal of schools within a three-state area.

Snow has become so scarce that weathermen, who work on a per-snow commission basis, have become desperate to the point of actually begging for snow.

All recent snows are measured against the Great Snow of 1927 when, according to how much caffeine the person telling the story has ingested that morning, it snowed from two to twenty-five feet deep.

The history of snow is spotty from that time until 1960, except that "we had a lot more snow back then." 1960, of course, was the famous "Three Wednesdays in a Row Snow." Another good snow worth repeating was the snow of 1989, which dumped fifteen inches on Wilmington. It is also worth noting that weathermen called for sunny and bright skies that day.

Our last really good snow (unless you believe that the only good snow is no snow) was in 1985 when it snowed knee-deep to Cynthia Smoot.

That was the snow that prompted us to buy boots for everyone in the family, boots that have long since dry rotted in the closet.

In North Carolina, it is wise to remember, you can have two-thirds of an inch of snow and a smidgen of ice and people will call it the worst December ever. You can easily be snowed in by a blizzard of a tenth of an inch.

You may also wonder how our weathermen make such pinpoint predications with only the aid of weather satellites, weather radar, Doppler radar, the entire National Weather service and voodoo to help them. I was able to document one such snow, now known as The Great Snow of 1993, to show you these professionals in action.

The storm had its beginnings in the Colorado Rockies where it dumped several feet of snow. Eagle-eyed weathermen watched this storm as it headed toward North Carolina and on February 23, began predicting that it would hit the Piedmont.

Wednesday, the 24th, weathermen everywhere in the Piedmont were boldly standing together behind the National Weather Service and were all predicting between four and six inches of snow.

Sometime during this period, Roy Ackland, perhaps sensing impending disaster, had himself admitted to a local hospital on the flimsy excuse of a burst appendix.

At noon on the 24th, schools from Murphy to Manteo, from Madison to Maxton, closed due to fear of snow. Problem is, there is no snow.

People began to remark that "it feels like snow." Birds begin to feed, "a sure sign of snow." Either that, or they're hungry. Travelers begin to call radio stations, reporting seeing "flakes."

Eric Chilton calls Roy Ackland at the hospital, where he is holed up with two loaves of bread and a gallon of milk. If those National Weather guys are pushing it, he says, it's bound to happen.

TV stations set up special phone lines with weather info and put all weathermen on 24 hour alert, sleeping in at the stations.

At 7 p.m. Frank Deal reports "no snow yet, but at 11:00 things will be totally different."

I am in the grocery store, bent over the ice cream cooler searching for cherry vanilla, when the news hits. Two thousand people clean out the bread section in fifteen seconds. The doctor says my bruises will heal up nicely, but I may suffer lingering psychological damage.

I panic when I see everyone going for the bread, grabbing bake and serve rolls, whole wheat bread and mini-donuts. If it is made from flour, it is gone. I manage to grab two loaves of bread and a can of Pillsbury Big Country Biscuits and don't lose but part of a thumb nail.

I get in line closer to my car than the cash register. Everyone is staring at me like part of my clothes are unzipped so I begin checking everything just to make sure it is still there. Finally the woman behind me informs me of my problem: I don't have any milk.

"Don't you know they're calling for snow?" she says politely.

I go back to the dairy case, but there is no milk left. Luckily, I find a box of Carnation Powered Milk and a couple of cans of Eagle Brand Milk instead.

Since I've lost my place in line, I take a chance on finding some toilet tissue. The only thing left is a 48-roll pack, so I throw this on the cart and go looking for some Hot Cocoa Mix and potato chips.

Upon arriving home, I find Sandra unloading her car. She has a long loaf of bread, three boxes of crackers, a gallon of milk, popcorn and forty-two cans of Campbell's chicken noodle soup.

"Don't you know they're calling for snow?" she says politely.

Two years later, we still have more powered milk than the Marine Corps.

At approximately 9 p.m. it begins to snow. At approximately 9:08, it stops. At 10:00, Frank Deal notes rather sheepishly that the storm seems to have passed us by and that "there is nothing behind it." A technician in the background laughs nervously.

Sometime during the night, freezing rain begins to fall, covering the trees and power lines.

The next day Randy Jackson explains the hazards of predicting snow in the Piedmont, acknowledging that it is easier to predict the weather in Peru.

Saturday, the 27th, sounds are heard throughout the

countryside: ice melting off the trees, bread men laughing all the way to the bank and weathermen chomping crow.

Grandma's Christmas Riches

In the vault of my mind that stores remembrances is housed recollections of tinsel and turkey and toys of many Christmases, all running together in a collage of memories. Intertwined within these memories is the realization that Christmas was, as we were growing up in Siler City, much more than fruits, nuts and candies. It was presents.

Of course, we marveled reverently at the story of the Christ Child, how Joseph and Mary were turned away at the inn and how the Baby Jesus was born in a manger. Deep down, though, we knew that had it not been for the fortunate arrival of the Wise Men and the later advent of Santa Claus, we would have been blessed with about as many toys as a tadpole.

It was not so much that we were poor, it was just that our parents, like most of our friends' parents, were stingy. We would have never, for example, gotten a new bicycle if we had to depend on our parents. They might have bought us a pair of blue jeans or a new tooth brush, but it was Santa Claus who brought the bicycles.

We were also pretty certain that Santa had something to do with the influx of candy into our homes around

Christmastime. This was a particularly amazing occurrence in a house where, throughout most of the year, the sweetest thing was a box of prunes.

We had a basic knowledge of economics at an early age. We were taught such things as money does not grow on trees, our parents were not made of money and that money is the root of all evil. This is mainly why none of it ever filtered down our way. Except at Christmas.

At first, we were kept in fear of Santa Claus by our parents as a futile attempt to control our behavior. Be good, our parents said, or Santa won't bring you any presents. After several Christmases of being our normal less than good selves, it soon occurred to us that no matter how we acted, short of armed robbery, we were going to get some loot.

Santa also became an unwitting accomplice to our parent's stinginess. We might feel an uncontrollable need, say, for a BB gun in June. Our parents would always answer "maybe Santa Claus will bring it to you". This seemed to be an unfair burden for Santa to bear, but it made our folks happy so we went along with it.

If we ever had any doubts as to the existence of Santa Claus, they were dispelled by our friend Willard. Willard confessed to us that there was bound to be a Santa Claus because his parents were too poor to afford all the luxuries that appeared under their tree every Christmas. Things were so tight at Willard's that, unusual as it sounds, Santa often bought clothes on Christmas.

The ultimate proof of the reality of Santa came on Willard's twelfth Christmas. It was on that Christmas that Willard found a brand new 20 gauge pump shotgun complete with a whole box of shells under his tree, much to the distress of his mother and most of the surrounding neighborhood. We all knew at that instant that Santa Claus really lived, a faith that has remained with us to this very day.

Christmas at our house generally started around 3 a.m. My brother and I would rather have slept later, but we felt an obligation to wake our parents and show them our gifts as early as possible. They were always appreciative and often showed their thanks by insisting we play outside with our toys, even in driving blizzards.

After playing awhile, we usually had a big Christmas dinner and then set off to our grandparents' houses, finally ending up at our grandmother's in Pittsboro that afternoon. Grandma was always glad to see all of us grandchildren, so much so that she too insisted that we play outside. This was especially true the year we all received cap pistols for Christmas.

Grandma lived in a modest frame house on the corner of Small Street and Highway 64, although Highway 64 had not always passed in front of her home. For years the road came in from Siler City, went three-quarters around the court house, then a few blocks north where it turned east again. When the highway was re-routed it went halfway around the courthouse and then directly east, right by Grandma's.

Re-routing the road brought Grandma insomnia, a few panhandlers and a rash of wrecks. We liked the road because we could stand in front of the house and by pumping our fist in the air we could get every transfer truck driver who passed to cut loose on his air horn. This feat would often bring Grandma out of her house and onto the porch where she would gesture wildly, a useless stunt, we thought, since the truck drivers couldn't even see her from there.

Grandma always had some small gift for us grand-children. It might be a pair of socks, a little something she had knitted or a book. One particularly lean Christmas, she gave me a few coils of rolled up pennies. It didn't take us long to figure out that you didn't get rich at Grandma's.

One of the first Christmases I remember is the Christmas of the fire. Wrapping paper thrown in the fireplace at Grandma's floated up the chimney, catching a bird's nest on fire and smoking up the living room. Although Santa had already come and gone and my presents were safely tucked away, I took no chances. I immediately blamed my brother for the fire. It didn't matter, for hordes of panicky adults were swarming around, looking for a phone to call the fire department and searching for an exit.

Here my memory varies slightly with that of those adults whose care I was in. My mother remembers bravely carrying me to safety, where I later deviously sneaked back into the house. I remember more clearly being left in the room with a cousin where we did the only rational thing left for two abandoned kids to do: we opened all the presents and threw the name tags into the fire.

Among all this Christmas glitter and leftovers of that day came an intrusion. We had all finally been herded inside with near frostbite after helping the firefighters by shooting at passersby with our cap pistols when the knock came at the door. A scruffy, shivering family stood on the front porch by the swing, a man, woman, small boy and little girl clinging to her mother.

My uncle answered the knock at the door, but Grandma soon came to see what the interruption was, wiping her hands on her apron. We had all gone to the window and saw the huddled family and heard our uncle tell them, yes, they could have some water for their radiator, when Grandma came to the porch.

She listened to the man as he told of how he had worked in a mill in Franklinville, but had been hurt and had not been able to work lately. The family had been to Raleigh to a sister's for Christmas and their car had broken down on the way home.

Grandma immediately ushered them inside and down the hallway past us wide-eyed grandchildren, to the den. There they gathered by the wood heater as Grandma uncovered the table. After they had eaten and were ready to leave, I saw one of those amazing miracles that are usually reserved for movies on TV. Everyone in my family, including my father who had to depend on Santa Claus to bring us a simple cowboy outfit, reached into their pockets and actually gave real money to these perfect strangers.

The next Christmas was the two-tree Christmas. This was the year that we hunted for hours over fence rows and broomstraw fields on Grandpa's farm to find the only cedar tree in Chatham County that had been urinated on by every deer and most of the raccoons in the neighborhood.

We hauled the tree home to the warmth of the house and trimmed it. Like most of the trees we cut for Christmas, it had grown considerably by the time we got it to the living room. It had also lost most of its shape, with one side having completely gone bald while we were carrying it home. This was the magic of cedar trees back then and once this tree warmed to room temperature, it began to reek a not so magical odor. We quickly untrimmed it and hauled it back outside to find a replacement.

As usual, this Christmas found us back at Grandma's. We had just finished defending the Alamo in the back bedroom, with the bed getting the worst of the attack, when the knock came at the front door. Our uncle went outside and closed the door behind him. Soon he was back.

"It's that same stranded family," he said incredulously. "They're out of gas this time. And money."

Well, I thought to myself, they've come to the right place. This family of mine who wouldn't even buy me a bow and arrow would donate their entire life savings to strangers. I had found that out last year.

Grandma let the family in over my uncle's protests and fed them. The rest of the family sulked in the living room, mumbling quietly among themselves.

When the stranded family was about to leave, I watched as Grandma opened the china cabinet and reached behind some dishes. I saw her pull out some bills and press them into the man's hand. At first he shook his head, but Grandma kept them there until he put them in his pocket.

Reality had thankfully set in with the rest of the family, however.

"I guess we might as well fix them a place at the table next Christmas," my father grumbled. "They're getting to be regulars."

"It's that new highway," my uncle said, "you don't know what dead beat is going to stop by next."

"I just hope they haven't stolen anything," an aunt said. "You just can't trust people nowadays."

"Oh, people are the same as they've always been,"

Grandma said. "They need help and if the highway brings them by, I'm going to help them."

Just to be sure, I checked my coonskin cap and rolls of pennies to see if they were still stashed under the bed.

The next Christmas was the one we almost moved out of the neighborhood. It was Mom who suggested the move and for quite some time she was adamant about it. Coincidentally, this was the Christmas Willard got the shotgun.

Again, we ended the day in Pittsboro. We had just finished Christmas supper at Grandma's when someone knocked at the front door. For a moment, all the adults just stared blankly at each other.

"You don't reckon it's that same stranded family again, do you?" my father asked. We kids giggled, but the adults evidently didn't see the humor.

Our uncle and Dad both went to the door, opened it and disappeared outside on the porch. We kids ran into the living room and pressed our faces against the window.

"It's them," I said. "It's that stranded family."

Grandma headed for the door. I could see Dad and my uncle talking animatedly to the man on the steps, while the woman and two children waited by the swing. Our uncle was saying something about taking advantage of an old woman's kindness when Grandma appeared on the porch.

"Well, hell-o," said Grandma like they were long lost friends. "Merry Christmas."

"Merry Christmas," said the woman, holding out a small gift wrapped package to Grandma. "We wanted you to have this for all your kindness. You see, John here is able to work now and I'm still taking in sewing. Times are better."

Grandma took the package.

"Won't ya'll come in?" she asked. "Out of the cold?"

No, said the woman, they had to be going. They just wanted to say thanks and Merry Christmas. And then the woman hugged Grandma.

Grandma came inside and unwrapped her present in silence. It was a hand crocheted star. Grandma fondled it awhile, then hung it on the top of the Christmas tree. Dad and my uncle were still outside, sitting on the steps.

I watched out the window as my breath fogged over the red tail lights from the traffic on the highway wondering what about a Christmas ornament could make Grandma cry.

It wasn't until several years later that I realized that perhaps you could get rich at Grandma's after all.

Willard and the Christmas Star

You may remember the night before Christmas several years ago when the temperature fell to around five degrees in Piedmont North Carolina. There weren't many of us creatures stirring throughout our house that Christmas Eve. We had all eaten a big meal and settled in for our traditional Christmas Eve ritual, known locally as Continuing to Gorge Ourselves Silly on Junk Food While Watching Old Christmas Movies Even Though We'd Seen Them 212 Times Already.

I was just about to stuff myself useless on more cookies when Sandra called me aside in the kitchen.

"Guess what?" she asked.

"You weren't able to rent *The Grinch Who Stole Christmas*," I moaned.

"No, we've forgotten the stocking stuffers," she whispered.

"I thought Santa was responsible for those," I whispered back.

"Well," she replied, "maybe you can help Santa out and ride downtown and get some before it gets dark and the stores close...just in case Santa runs out before he gets here."

Santa had often run low of provisions just before arriving at our house, so it seemed logical to help him out. Sometimes Santa needs all the help he can get. Besides, I could stop at the video store and pick up *The Chipmunk's Christmas* before they closed. We'd only seen it 211 times.

I threw on a coat, grabbed a large handful of cookies to munch on along the way, bid *Scrooge* good-by and headed for the car. As I rounded the corner of the house, the wind was so cold I had to look down to see if I still had pants on. Luckily, I did. But when I looked back up, unluckily my old friends Willard and Hoyle were pulling into the driveway in Willard's truck with the dogbox on the back.

Willard and Hoyle have been my best friends since the third grade, a point in their lives when they reached the peak of their intellectual development.

"Where're you going?" Willard asked, rolling down his window about a quarter of an inch against the bitter cold.

I told him about the stocking stuffers.

"Hop in," he said. "Me and Hoyle, we got to go down to the store, too. Got to pick up some presents 'cause tomorrow's Christmas. We been out all afternoon looking for Gypsy."

Against all hope of ever seeing home again before New Year's, I crawled in beside Hoyle. He and Willard had been coon hunting the night before and couldn't find Willard's Blue Tick hound, Gypsy. This wasn't an unusual occurrence since Gypsy would rather do anything than coon hunt. She would trail deer, possum, rabbits, fox and tom cats, but showed a general disdain for coons. Gypsy, I figured, was at this very moment playing in a backyard with someone's kids.

Willard had never given up on Gypsy, although Hoyle, being a Black and Tan man, had encouraged him to. I sided with Gypsy when it came to coon hunting, having numerous times been smacked in the face with a gracious plenty of sweet gum limbs while wandering around in the dark chasing howling hound dogs.

"So when did you guys decide it was Christmas?" I asked as we neared the store.

"Oh, we've known for several days, now," said Hoyle, "we just been busy coon hunting."

"Yeah," said Willard, "we don't like to start shopping too early. It ruins your Christmas spirit."

Christmas Eve is a good time to shop. The stores aren't too crowded with shoppers, the salespeople are too worn to a frazzle to talk back to you and there is not enough merchandise left on the shelves to be confusing.

I picked up some fruits and nuts and candies for Julie and Jamie's stockings. Willard bought a sled for one nephew, a truck for another and a small train set for yet another. Hoyle picked up some Barbie dolls, a doll house, a small toy cook stove and a 21-piece tea set for his girls. For good measure, and because he knew no one else would buy him one, Willard bought himself a Tree Brand pocket knife.

"That's good, Willard," Hoyle laughed when we got to the truck. "Got your nephew a sled and it ain't snowed in a hundred years around here."

"He's dreaming of a white Christmas," growled Willard as he pulled out of the parking lot in the opposite direction of my house.

"Hey, I'm missing *The Grinch*," I yelled. "The last time you did this to me we ended up in Kentucky. Besides, I'm almost out of cookies."

"I'm gonna go back one more time and see if I can't find Gypsy," Willard promised, "then I'll get you home."

Willard turned off the paved road onto a dirt road, then onto another dirt road. By then it was 6:00 and pretty dark. At the bottom of the hill at the darkest part of the woods, he cut off his motor and called Gypsy.

"We didn't come this far last night," grumbled Hoyle.

"Yeah we did," countered Willard, "right down there is where you tripped over that old bob wire."

"Oh, yeah," Hoyle said, rubbing his head. The cold began to infiltrate our flimsy clothes as the heat left the truck cab. Willard ground the ignition of the old truck. It wouldn't start.

Hoyle said it was the battery and Willard said it was the ignition. He'd been meaning to replace it. I mumbled something to the effect that it was just the luck, or the un-luck, of being with them at a given moment because I knew something like this was bound to happen.

Hoyle got out and lifted the hood and jiggled the battery cables and Willard ground the starter again. Nothing happened. That's when we all noticed the light.

On the top of a hill across the valley and down the road from the direction we'd just driven a bright star lit up an old farm house.

"I didn't notice no house back there," said Hoyle.

"Must be a Christmas decoration on top of the house," said Willard. "Let's go up there and call someone to come get us before we freeze to death."

It looked like a real star to me, but before I could suggest we look for a driveway, Willard and Hoyle had headed out through the woods. The valley turned out to be a frozen swamp edged with about two acres of briars and honeysuckles. I heard something go "sprang" about the time I stepped into a rotted stump hole and heard Hoyle cuss.

"This is the place all right," he said. "I found that bob wire fence again."

About that time a sweet gum branch slapped me square in the face stinging so badly my eyes watered.

Finally we reached the house. A tom cat flew by us and I could swear I heard the familiar excited chop of a Blue Tick hound close on a warm trail. A star lit up the whole yard and most of the barn and I could see that Willard's head was so peppered with cockleburrs and beggar's lice that he looked like a Chia Pet. Hoyle didn't look much better.

Willard knocked on the door and an old man finally opened it.

"Sir, our truck has knocked off down at the road and we followed your star through the swamp hoping we could use your phone," said Willard, wrapping his arms around himself trying to get warm.

"Come on in," the old man said, hospitably holding the door open. "Milly," he yelled, "there's three wise men out here what have been following a star. Well, two wise men," he said after glancing at Willard's cockleburr covered cap again.

"Why didn't ya'll come up the driveway?" he asked.

"Grandpa, I told you not to let strangers in the house," said a smallish woman peering from the darkness of the living room where a wood stove burned. It was a neat house, I noticed, but bare of everything but necessities. "We don't have no phone, we don't have no car," she continued, "and I'm afraid we can't help you. I'd appreciate it if you'd leave."

A little cherub-faced boy and pixie girl peeked out around the corner.

"Is it Santa Claus?" the little girl asked.

"I told ya'll Santa Claus wouldn't be stopping here this year," the mother said softly. "Now get back to your rooms."

"If Harvey hadn't got to drinking and run off, it wouldn't be like this," the old man said.

"Don't pay any attention to Grandpa," the woman said. "He was hurt in the war and ain't been right since."

"Fell off the Army's turnip truck," mumbled Willard.

"I hope you ain't put no star on top of the house," the old man said to the woman. "It'll attract shepherds and their flocks and all sorts of weirdos." He looked right at Willard.

"You know we can't afford no decorations," she answered. "Sorry we can't help ya'll," she said, looking back at us. "The Fergusons live down the road. They have a phone."

We went back out in the cold and as we walked down the hill I looked back to see the star on the house. All I could see was the moon shining off the tin roof.

"That old man was missing a couple of eggs out of his egg nog," griped Willard, limping down the driveway. "I called him Methuselah and he kicked me in the shin. I believe he's about a yule log shy of a load."

"Let's try the truck one more time before we walk any farther," I suggested, my teeth chattering. "Maybe it's just flooded."

Willard gave me that crazy look of his, but got in the cab and tried it anyway. The truck cranked right up. As we sat there soaking up the warmth of the heater, we all knew what we had to do. After we'd gotten good and warm, we pulled all the presents out of the bed of the truck and hauled them back up the hill to the house, except this time we used the driveway. Willard arranged them on the front porch.

It took some explaining to convince Sandra what actually had happened, but she already knew about the Kentucky trip and that made it easier. I made Hoyle and Willard come in and collaborate my story, although they were less than credible witnesses and may even have hindered matters somewhat by tracking beggar's lice and leaves on the carpet.

None of us suffered that Christmas. The nephews got more presents than ever, Hoyle's daughters had plenty and somehow that Christmas morning we awoke to find all our stockings stuffed.

I heard years later that Millie had awoken early that Christmas morning unable to sleep because of either a bright star or the light of the moon shining off the tin roof of the barn. She had seen the presents on the porch and placed them under the tree just before the children awoke. The old man had really liked his Tree Brand knife and the children their toys. But it was said that the woman was particularly thankful for the Blue Tick hound she found sleeping on the sled that morning, a dog that was especially playful with the children and watchful of weirdos who might sneak up to the house from the swamp.

My Yule Log

Christmas always sneaks up on us. It's like winter: you know it's coming every year, but it's still a surprise.

Last year, I made a vow to get a better grasp on Christmas, to lasso and hog-tie it, so to speak, so that it doesn't trample me to smithereens as it has done in the past. So I began a Christmas diary right after Christmas last year in an attempt to stop things from snowballing on me and to figure out just when Christmas starts and when it ends. Here is part of that diary:

December 26: Purchase bows, Christmas cards, name tags and wrapping paper on sale. Get considerable bargain on wrapping paper, two rolls for $5. Add it to the other 23 rolls in the attic, some of which are beginning to dry rot. Realize that December 26 is actually first Christmas shopping day of the year.

December 27: Find the same shirts purchased for brother for Christmas at $25 each, now on sale for $10. Buy two for him for next Christmas

March 25: Complete stranger on street remarks to no one in particular "only nine more months till Christmas." Police prevent mob from seriously harming him.

May 14: Wife discovers "Christmas House" in

Dillsboro, an entire house devoted solely to Christmas decorations and other Christmas related items. Reminds me of our house on Christmas Eve, except we have more stuff. Wife decides to buy numerous gifts to give to friends at Christmas, including ample candles for our own use.

May 15: Candles melt in trunk on way home.

June 25: Finally finish off last of nine fruitcakes. Have to cut last one with a hatchet. Go to store to try to find another one. Clerk greets me with "only six more months till Christmas!"

July 3: Notice that Wal-Mart has its Christmas material displayed in fabric section.

July 5: Heilig Meyers announces its "Christmas in July" sale.

August 1: Comic strip "The Family Circus": Boy is looking up at sky and saying "if summer had Christmas, it would be perfect."

September 25: Spot sign in jewelry store window: "Only 91 more days left until Christmas."

October 1: Last day to mail package by boat to Zimbabwe and expect to get it there by Christmas.

October 2: Respond to TV ad and order Giant Christmas Musical Anthology of 90 Christmas songs on four long-playing cassettes, few of which are by the original artists and some of which are actually in English, for only $34.95.

October 3: Wife finds exact same tapes in Wal-Mart for $9.95.

October 21: Christmas stamps go on sale at post office. Clerk overheard asking lady if she'd like a Madonna stamp. Lady says even though that is son's favorite singer, she personally doesn't care for her.

November 1: Great deluge of Christmas advertising begins with Christmas savings sales and pre-holiday sales. Stores offer same wrapping paper I bought last December at three rolls for $5. I buy three rolls just in case.

November 2: Belk Yates offers temporary jobs as sales associates "during the fun-filled Christmas season." The ad says: "Feel the excitement of Christmas." Having worked many Christmases in my youth as a sales associate in various retail stores, I have immediate flashbacks, causing shins to ache where old ladies fighting over specials kicked me. Doctor diagnoses as Post Traumatic Retail Store Stress Syndrome.

November 5: Local stores begin displaying fruitcake ingredients and eggnog.

November 6: Entry in diary smudged by what appears to be eggnog.

November 7: Christmas catalog arrives advertising "Mr. Christmas", a 7-foot tall Oregon pine Christmas tree with real wood-like trunk and stand for only $89.99. Wife, remembering last year's "Battle of the Tree", suggests we buy one. I convince her that this year I will subdue the live tree into its tree stand without chopping it into kindling.

November 8: Exotic beetles are reported to have munched their way onto Christmas tree farms and are stunting growth of trees in the Great Lakes area. I envision live trees costing hundreds of dollars. Order "Mr. Christmas."

November 9: Wife invites several friends over to make Christmas angel decorations out of palm leaf fans. This involves glue guns, palm leaf fans, angel heads, about forty dollars worth of hair, some sparklie stuff and eyeballs.

November 10: For only about a hundred dollars we

have two creatures closely resembling Little Orphan Annie angels, a carpet full of glue and sparklie stuff and one slightly hung over wife who stood over glue gun too long.

November 17: Calvin, of comic strip fame, is kicked out of the house by his mom after singing a Christmas carol. He shouts, "Not thinking about it won't make it go away, you know."

November 18: A thief steals Christmas gifts from a house in High Point, unwrapping them first. Who would wrap presents so early?

November 19: Help wife wrap presents. Cannot find shirts bought for brother December 26.

November 20: Wife decides to use stuff purchased at Christmas House for herself.

November 22: Lowes begins selling Christmas trees.

November 24: Thanksgiving: I ask wife "Why can't we celebrate Thanksgiving before we get started on Christmas?" She smiles and continues making Santa Clauses out of yarn and Clorox bottles.

November 25: Day after Thanksgiving: We head for mall for Day After Thanksgiving Official First Day of Christmas Shopping and Demolition Derby. Find two shirts for brother at $30 a piece.

Ah, Christmas! My favorite year of time.

Cheeto's Christmas

We'd just returned home Thanksgiving night when the doorbell rang. It was Alfredo Cheeto Mascara, an old friend from Tibet. He was on his way to Washington to lobby Congress for foreign aid to compensate for Tibet's recent sweet potato blight.

We talked Cheeto into staying with us for a few days. Being new in America, Cheeto was very interested in our way of life. He knew that we Americans embody cultivation and sophistication known and admired throughout the world and wanted to visit one of our cultural centers. So I decided to take him to the mall.

The day after Thanksgiving marks the beginning of the holiday season, I told Cheeto. The Friday after Thanksgiving is the official start of Christmas.

Cheeto wanted to know what Christmas was. The only holiday they have in Tibet, he said, is Groundhog Day and he said if it wasn't for hiding the eggs, even that wouldn't be any fun.

I told him Christmas is the time we celebrate the birth of Christ. It is a time of joy, of hope, of peace on Earth and goodwill toward men.

What about women, Cheeto wanted to know. Didn't

they get any of this goodwill?

The women get the biggest dose of all, I told him.

The greatest part of Christmas is the spirit of giving you find all across America, I told Cheeto. Everyone buys presents for their friends and loved ones and the day after Thanksgiving kicks it all off.

Cheeto wanted to get in on all this joy and goodwill, so we got up early that Friday to get a good start. At first Cheeto didn't want to put on the shin guards, but I convinced him to by showing him the scars I got at the mall last year. It wasn't so hard to get him to wear the blaze orange jump suit when I told him we could easily get run over without it.

We hit a massive traffic jam about five miles from the mall. Cheeto remarked that a great many people seemed to be possessed with the Christmas spirit.

Some poor guy's car had stalled in our lane and steam was pouring out the open hood. Other drivers began to comment on the situation.

"What does 'stupid jerk' mean?" asked Cheeto. "Is that some kind of Christmas greeting?"

"Not exactly," I said, "some pagans must have worked their way into this line."

Little by little I edged our car into the other lane, almost hitting several other cars.

"What is that hand gesture people keep giving you?" Cheeto asked. "It looks similar to the one-fingered salute we have in Tibet."

"It's an old American custom," I explained. "It means 'well done, fellow traveler'."

"Aren't you going to stop and help the man with the stalled car?" Cheeto asked.

"No time," I told him. "We've got to get to the mall

to buy Christmas presents and to spread Christmas cheer."

"Aren't you going to let any of those other cars in this lane with you?" Cheeto wanted to know.

"It's every man for himself in this world," I told him.

As we were waiting in traffic, I taught Cheeto several America phrases I thought would be valuable to him once we reached the mall: "Charge it", "It's not my fault" and "Don't shoot, you can have the money."

Finally we made it into the mall parking lot and joined a mass of cars churning around looking for a parking place. I spotted one and we dueled two old ladies in a Volkswagen for it. We would have had it, too, had not a mother pushing a baby carriage gotten in the way. Cheeto hollered at her. He was really getting into this spirit thing. The two old ladies thumbed their credit cards at us.

We finally outraced an invalid man and his arthritic wife for a parking space.

"Lock the doors," I told Cheeto. "People will steal the socks off you this time of year."

"I just love this holiday of yours," said Cheeto, after we'd got inside the mall. "I can just feel the spirit of giving and the joy and the hope of big savings in the air. Now, how do we get one of these salespeople to help us?"

"We don't," I explained. "They're just here to guard the counter and to process our credit card purchases and to make sure we don't shoplift anything."

An elderly woman dropped her package and Cheeto started to help her pick it up. She began flailing him with her cane. While we were getting them untangled, someone picked Cheeto's pocket and stole his billfold.

"That's Ok," he said, "they just got cash. I've still got my credit cards. Now, tell me about this holiday of yours, again," he said, rubbing his head. "I'm slightly confused."

"Christmas," I said, "is all about peace and love and giving. It's the biggest holiday in the Christian world. We buy each other gifts, send cards, put up Christmas trees and decorate them lavishly. It's the one day of the year we feed the hungry and homeless and in some parts of the country, people actually speak to strangers on the street. Santa Claus and eight tiny reindeer bring presents made by elves for all the children.

"We sing songs about Rudolph and Frosty the Snowman. If Christmas ever falls on a Sunday, churches even cancel their services in honor of it," I continued.

"All this kindness sort of stresses us out so badly that we are usually beat down physically and mentally by the time Christmas gets here and we are actually glad when it's over.

"But it's wonderful fun," I added.

"No wonder everyone's so mad," said Cheeto.

I asked Cheeto if he thought Tibet would like a holiday like Christmas.

"It reminds me of an old Tibet tradition called 'Civil War' ", he said, "but I don't think we're ready for it. I don't think we have the patience for all this good will."

A Tree By Any Other Name Would Be Just As Crooked

By now you've probably encountered the single most stressful time in your marriage, that of decorating the Christmas tree.

Some of you have probably weaseled out of this sacred duty by feigning hunger and running out to get a pizza while your spouse finishes the job. Others of you have purchased an artificial tree and thus have eliminated most of the fun of Christmas, that of putting up a live (or, in some cases, a dead) tree in a stand.

While doing some early Christmas shopping, Sandra had noticed a space aged looking Christmas tree stand, an amazingly simple concoction which would readily accept any size tree up to and including a large oak.

"Why don't we get one of those," she remarked naively, "and cut out some of the hassle of trying to fit a tree into that old stand of yours."

I reminded her that what she termed as a hassle was an old cherished part of Christmas, a tradition carried on for years and one that I looked forward to annually with great anticipation.

I also reminded her that what she referred to as "that old stand of yours" was actually a 1959 red and green Rose's model tree stand made out of real metal and not this phoney plastic stuff you find in stores nowadays.

Once, years ago before metal was invented, we went out into the woods to find the perfect tree, one that after we had finally dragged it home, had grown two feet higher than the ceiling. There was no fun in this exercise, however, because when we got the tree home, we just cut the top out of it, nailed two boards on the bottom, set it in the corner and covered all its defects with massive amounts of icicles.

Now we prefer to go out and buy our tree rather than cutting one. We do this to help the economy and to prevent any trespassing charges which might ensue. We don't like artificial trees because we like the smell of a dead one.

One year we made the mistake of buying a tree that already had the stand attached, which took much of the fun out of the tree. This year I wanted a tree that I could put in our old tree stand, just like old times.

While shopping in Greensboro and dodging many shoppers, mostly men with vacant stares on their faces, we spotted a lot filled with trees. As a matter of fact, every lot we spotted was filled with Christmas trees, including every grocery store lot, funeral home, pasture, church yard, beer joint and some pool halls.

We pulled into the lot and picked out a nicely shaped, medium sized tree which cost slightly more than my first house payment.

A small, wiry lady hopped out to help us, put an oversized pair of gloves on and grabbed the tree, hauled it over to a table where a chain saw awaited.

"What kind of stand do you have?" she asked. "I'll trim it to fit."

"Well, actually," I said, "you see, we have this antique tree stand and I'd rather just trim it myself, which is sort of a tradition every year for us and one that we'd rather not give up because it brings us so much joy."

"Oh," she replied, "you've got one of those old rusty Rose's stands. You ought to get one of those new plastic ones."

"You should have let her trim it," said Sandra on the way home. "It would save you a lot of hassle."

"I wasn't about to let Chainsaw Charlene mess up our tree," I replied. "Besides, it's a tradition, not a hassle."

Once home, I began trimming the trunk of the tree with a hand saw to fit our stand (thus the origin of the phrase "trimming the tree") while Sandra began the two most important aspects of decorating a tree: 1. Finding the decorations 2. Untangling the lights.

I soon realized that our small, slim tree had the trunk of a redwood and our tree stand had the opening of a corn stalk. It also soon became apparent that the temperature on the deck where I was trimming the tree was approaching zero faster than I could trim. It was also apparent that Sandra was not going to let me cut the tree in the den or even in the living room.

After about a hour of cutting, chopping, whacking and coercing, intermingled with trips inside to warm my hands and aggravate Sandra, I managed to force the tree into the stand.

I carried it into the house and stood it in the corner. It closely resembled the Leaning Tower of Pisa. Finally after trimming it some more, straightening out a bent leg on the stand, hammering another side of the stand and then placing wood chips in strategic places under one leg, the tree stood straight.

"It'll be fine as long as you don't touch it," I told Sandra.

"Why don't you go get us some pizza while I decorate the tree?" she suggested.

Christmas is Giving

There was nothing significant about the Christmas that would bring back any memory for me.

Obviously Willard remembered it, but I had no reason to. It was a Christmas that had run together with other Christmases past, a blur of red and gold and green in my mind.

The story can finally be told now because some of the participants have passed away. And Willard has said that there is nothing else I can tell about him any more damaging than what I have already written in the past.

You can always spot photos of the '70's. I cringe every time I see those pictures of Willard and me, the bell bottoms, the long sideburns, Willard with the beard. But Aunt Maude almost always looks the same in all her photos, prim and proper, not much for foolishness.

That's why it bothered her so when Willard moved in beside her. Here she was, widow of the war hero, a lady who had lived by herself in the same neat house ever since World War II, a person who donated her time to causes and charities, who belonged to the American Legion auxiliary, the VFW, the DAR. If it had initials, she belonged to it. She was a lady of dignity in a quiet neighborhood, both aging gracefully together.

Willard shattered all that. He rented the old house beside Aunt Maude that summer and immediately disrupted her life. Willard's car had done that when he pulled into the driveway that day with the peace symbols on the back glass and the sticker on the bumper that read "Hell No I Won't Go."

He had spotted Aunt Maude staring out her bedroom window at him and flashed her the peace sign. Their relationship had gone down hill from there.

Aunt Maude was not an easy woman to get to know and Willard never got a foot in the door. I remembered being ill at ease in her home. It seemed almost sterile to me as a kid, and I never felt comfortable there. She had her late husband's medals in a frame in the den, I remember, and covers on all the furniture in the living room. A cross stitch in a frame in her den also stuck in my mind, a quote by Emerson. "The only gift is of thyself," it read.

I once bragged to Aunt Maude of the presents Santa was bringing me one Christmas.

"Life," she chided me, "is not about getting. It's about giving."

When I told her I was starting a coin collection, she took me into her bedroom to a desk where she had stored several sheets of stamps, stationery and a few coins her husband had brought back from overseas.

Some of the stamps, she said, were from the war, and she saved them to remember. Others were purchased years ago, and she still used them, like the five-cent stamps with the angel blowing the trumpet. She thought they were pretty and stuck two on a letter now and then.

She gave me the coins to put in my collection, and

I made a mental note to buy her some pretty stamps sometime.

Willard had managed to come out of the '60s and into the '70s an old hippie. He had avoided the Vietnam War like the plague. He stayed in college as long as he could and when it looked like he was going to be drafted, he married Lorena, the lady wrestler from Coleridge.

Now, with the war over, he was happily divorced and working at a nearby plant, partying at night and, in general, aggravating Aunt Maude to death.

The last straw, for Aunt Maude at least, came on a Wednesday when during one of Aunt Maude's many ladies auxiliary meetings, Willard mooned the entire membership of the local VFW post.

I had tried, to no avail, to assure Aunt Maude that it was two pumpkins she had seen in Willard's window, but she wouldn't buy it. Besides, she had witnesses, many it seemed who had been mooned before and were familiar with the phenomenon.

So, it was no surprise that Aunt Maude was discussing erecting a fence between her house and Willard when word came that Willard had been laid off at the factory.

The layoffs came at a bad time, right at Christmas, but the recession had forced many plants to cut back on their operations. Willard told me that he would probably have to move back in with his parents, which was somewhat tantamount to entering prison.

But Willard never moved. And in spite of being out of work that Christmas, he seemed to prosper. Well, not exactly prosper, but he did manage to make it through the winter to spring, when he found a job selling auto parts.

And he bought Christmas presents for everyone,

including Hoyle and me, something he'd never done, and he was even spotted dropping some money into the Salvation Army bucket one night.

Hoyle figured that Willard had committed robbery, but I surmised that his parents had bankrolled him through the hard times rather than have him move back home. All Willard said was that he'd received a loan.

Willard seemed to mature after that Christmas and it was quieter in the neighborhood. He trimmed his beard and actually mowed his yard occasionally. He was still Willard, of course, but I thought he had become more generous. He and Aunt Maude never got along, but they tolerated each other until her death several Christmases later.

A couple of years after that, Willard moved out of the old house to the other side of town, and I was helping him load his stuff into the U-Haul-it.

One box in particular caught my eye when I saw several business sized envelopes sticking out of it.

"Willard," I said, "you've saved everything you've ever owned."

"That's my letters from my Christmas Angel," he replied. "I save them to remind me to repay my loan."

He could tell I was perplexed by the look on my face.

"I got this money in the mail when I was out of work. I never knew who sent it," he said, holding up five or six envelopes.

"How are you going to pay it back if you don't know who sent it?" I asked.

"Oh, the person said just to help someone else in need. That's how you pay it back."

I looked down at the box with the long envelopes, each bearing two five-cent Christmas stamps with an angel blowing a trumpet.

"Yeah," I replied, "life isn't about getting. It's about giving."

It was all I could say, but somehow it seemed enough.